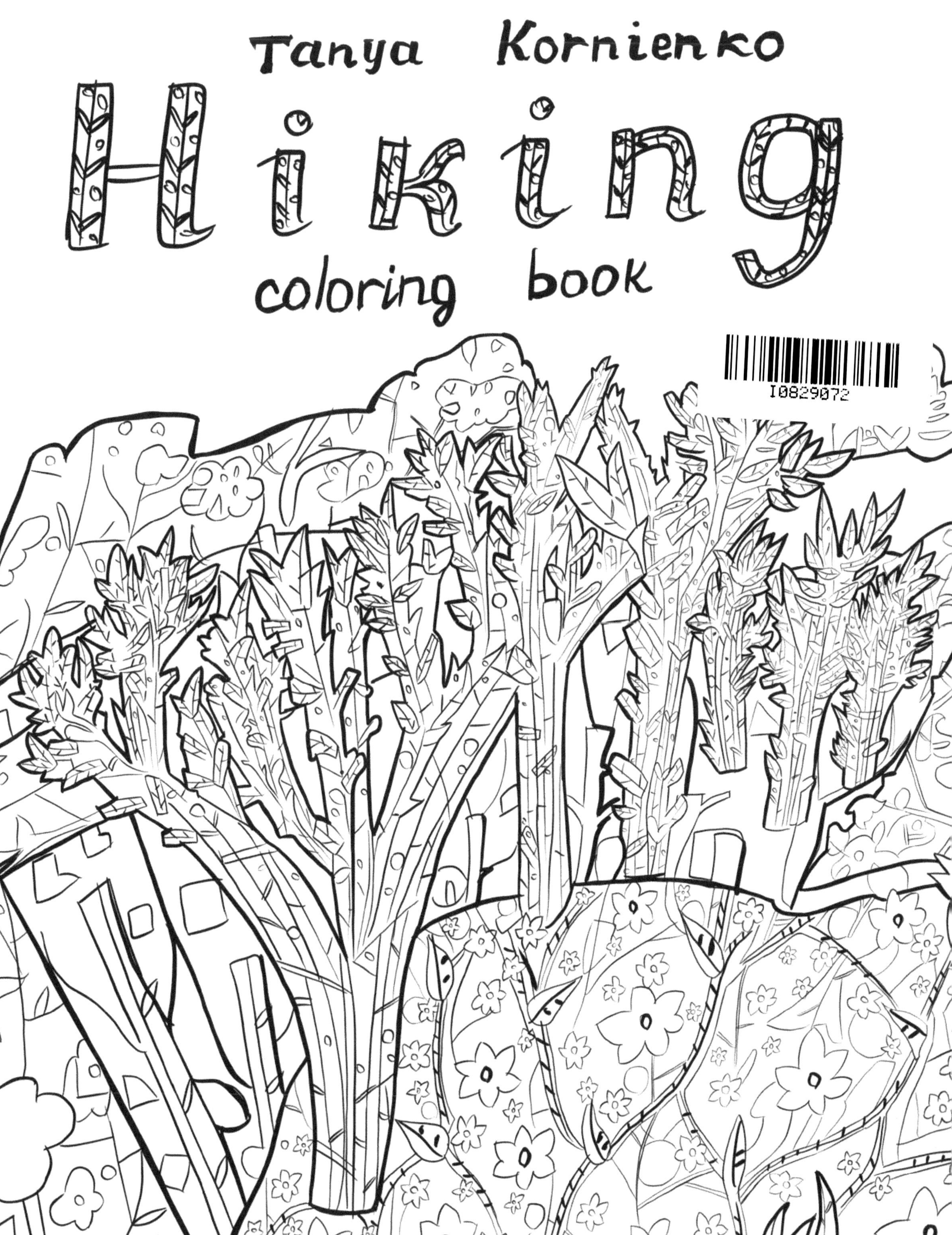
Tanya Kornienko
Hiking
coloring book
I0829072

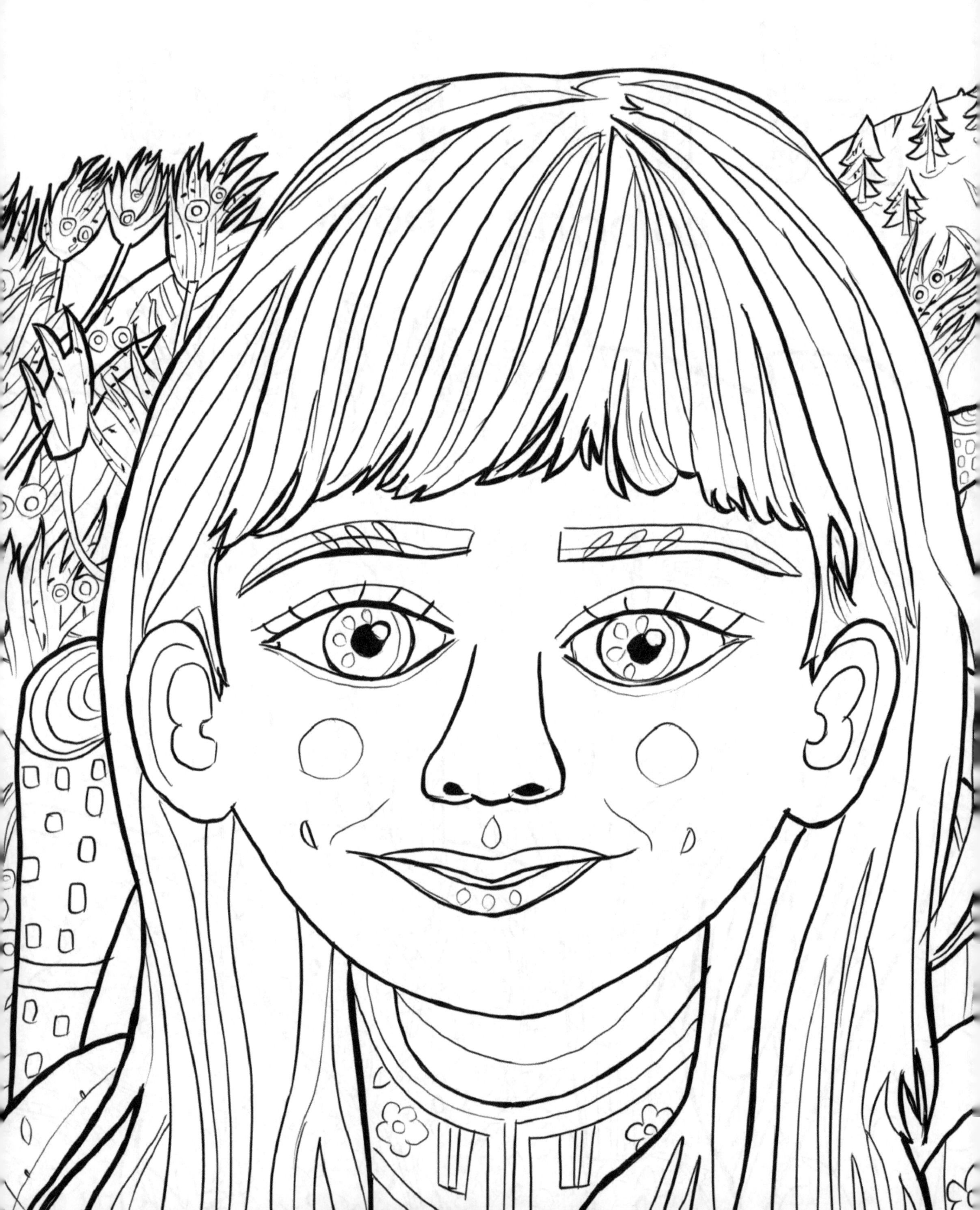

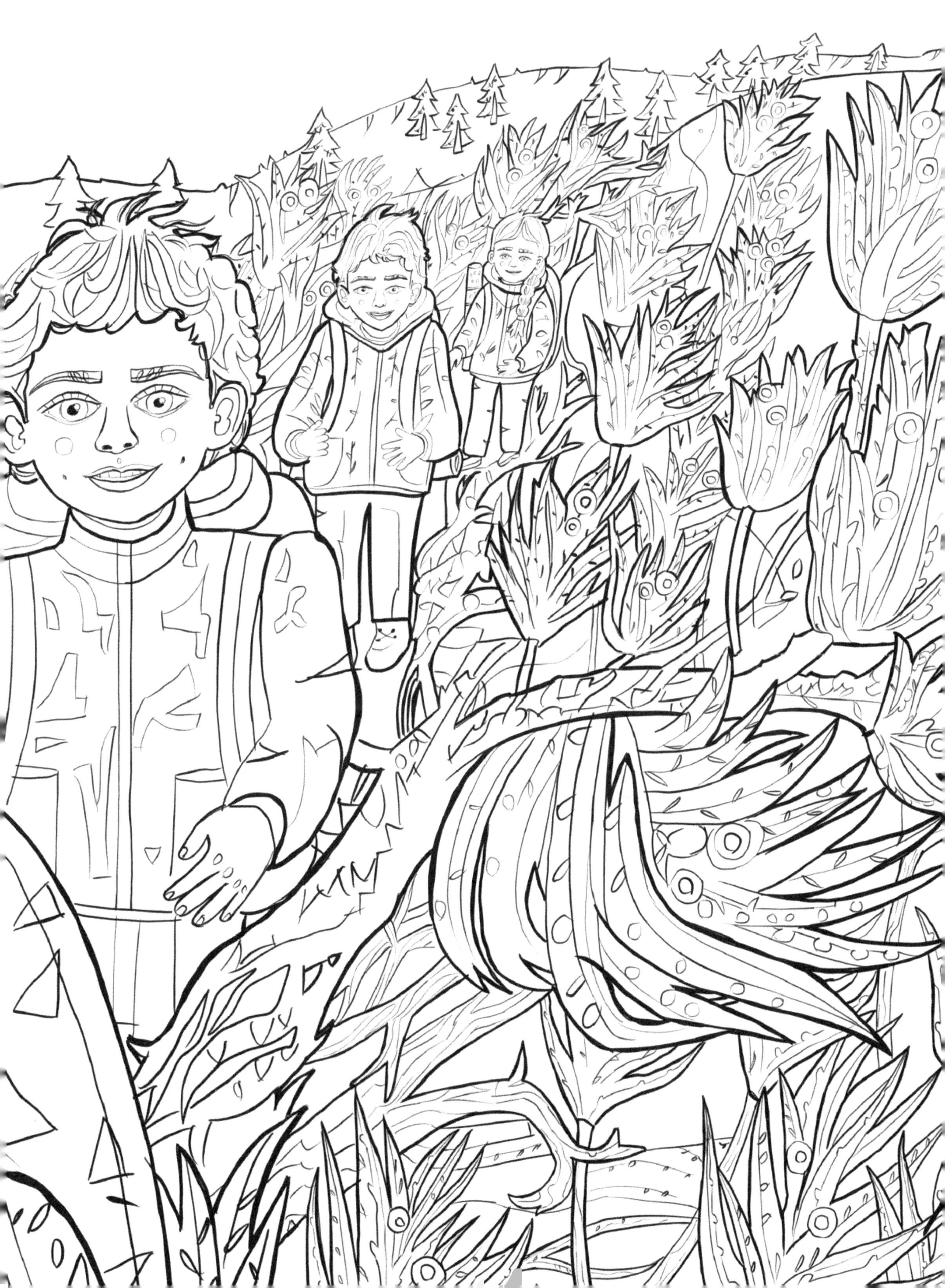

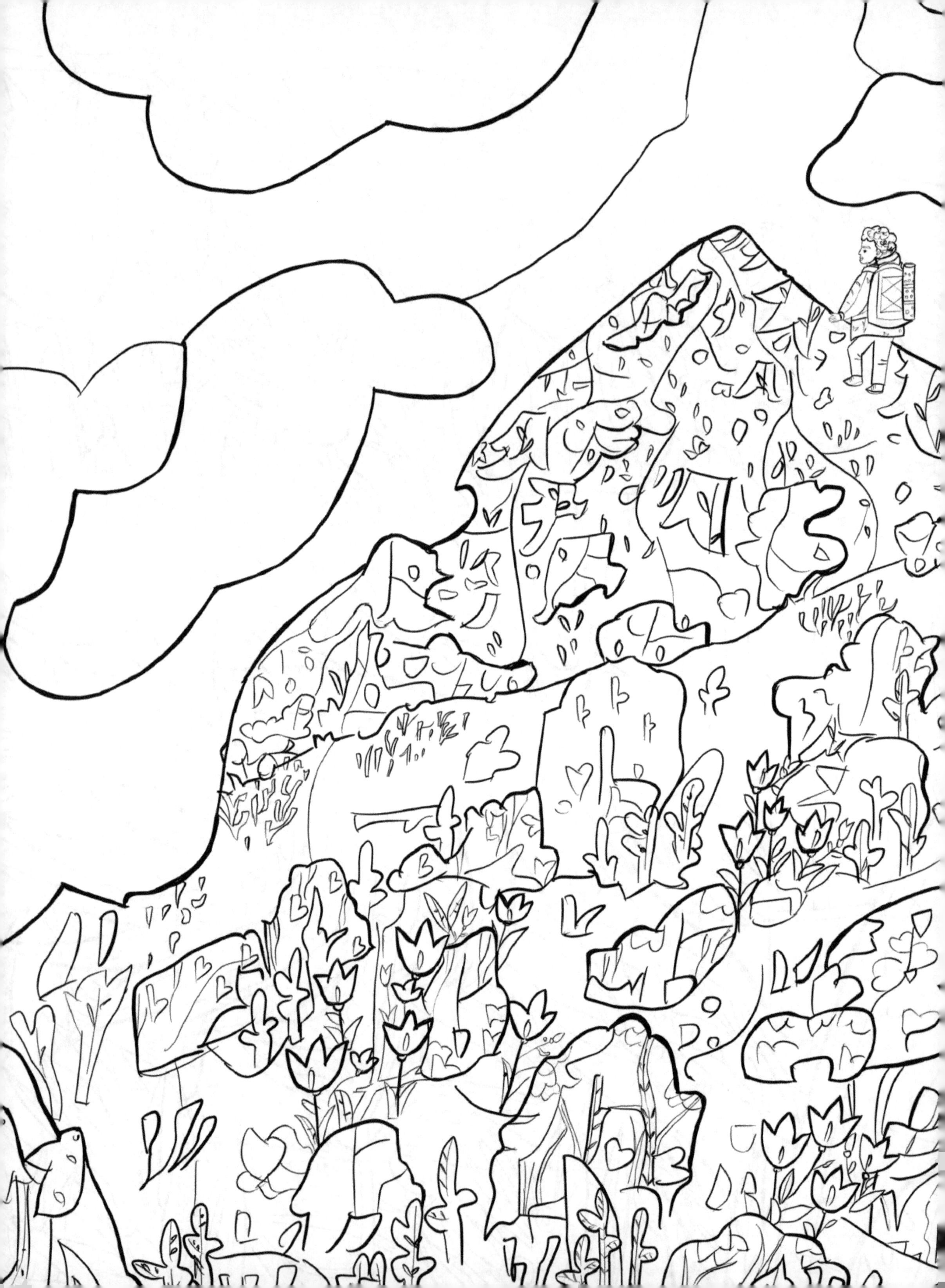

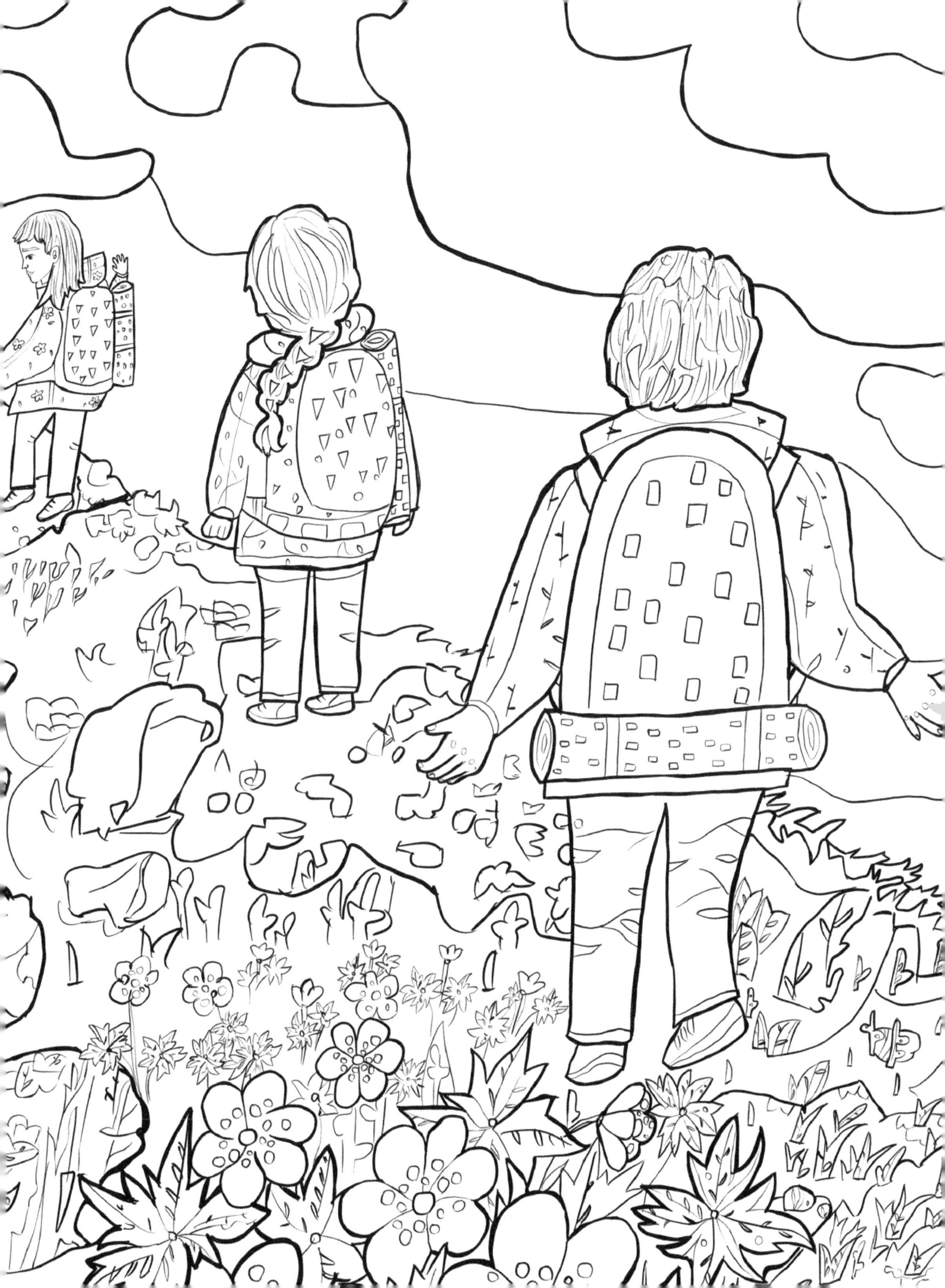

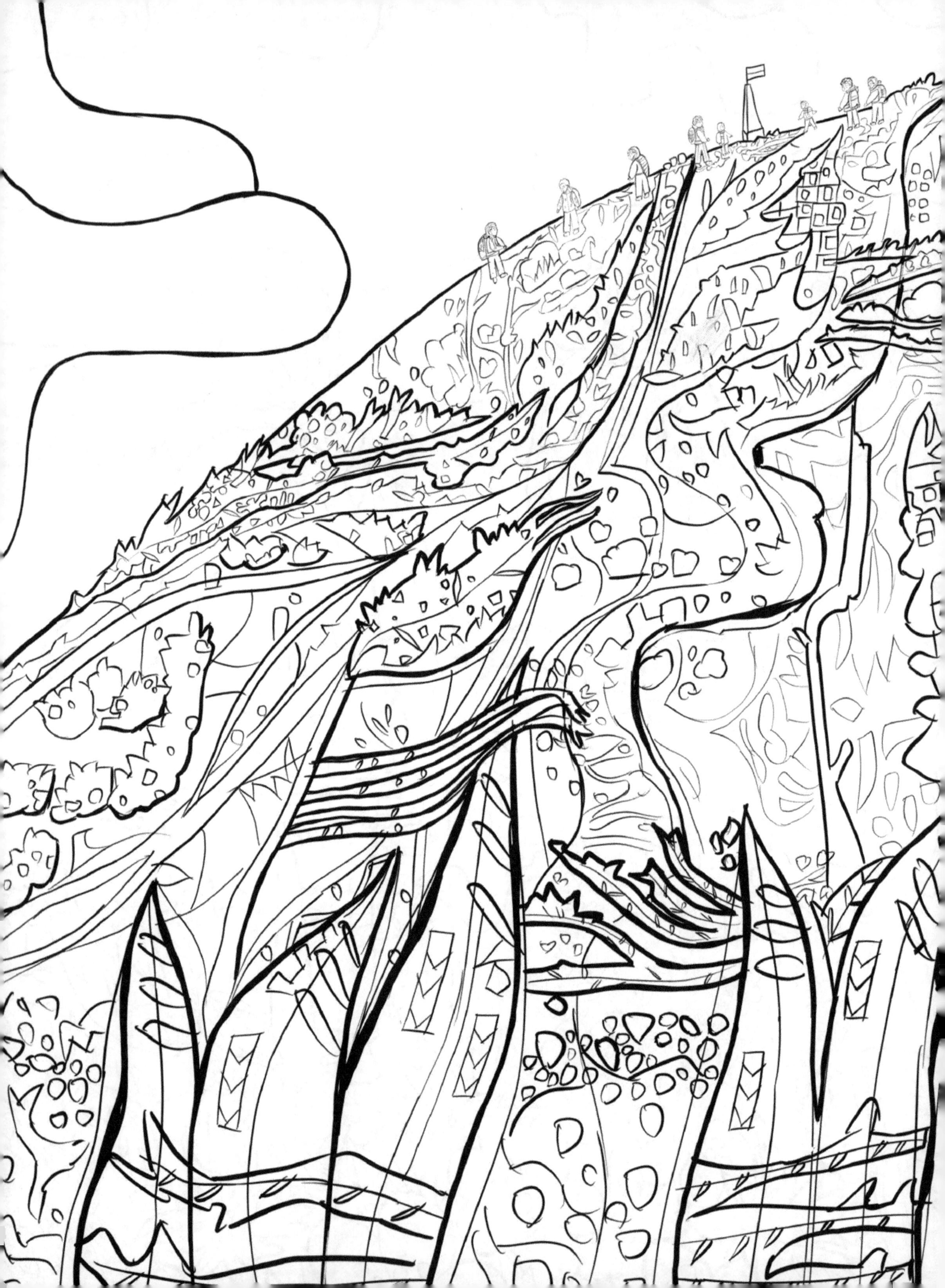

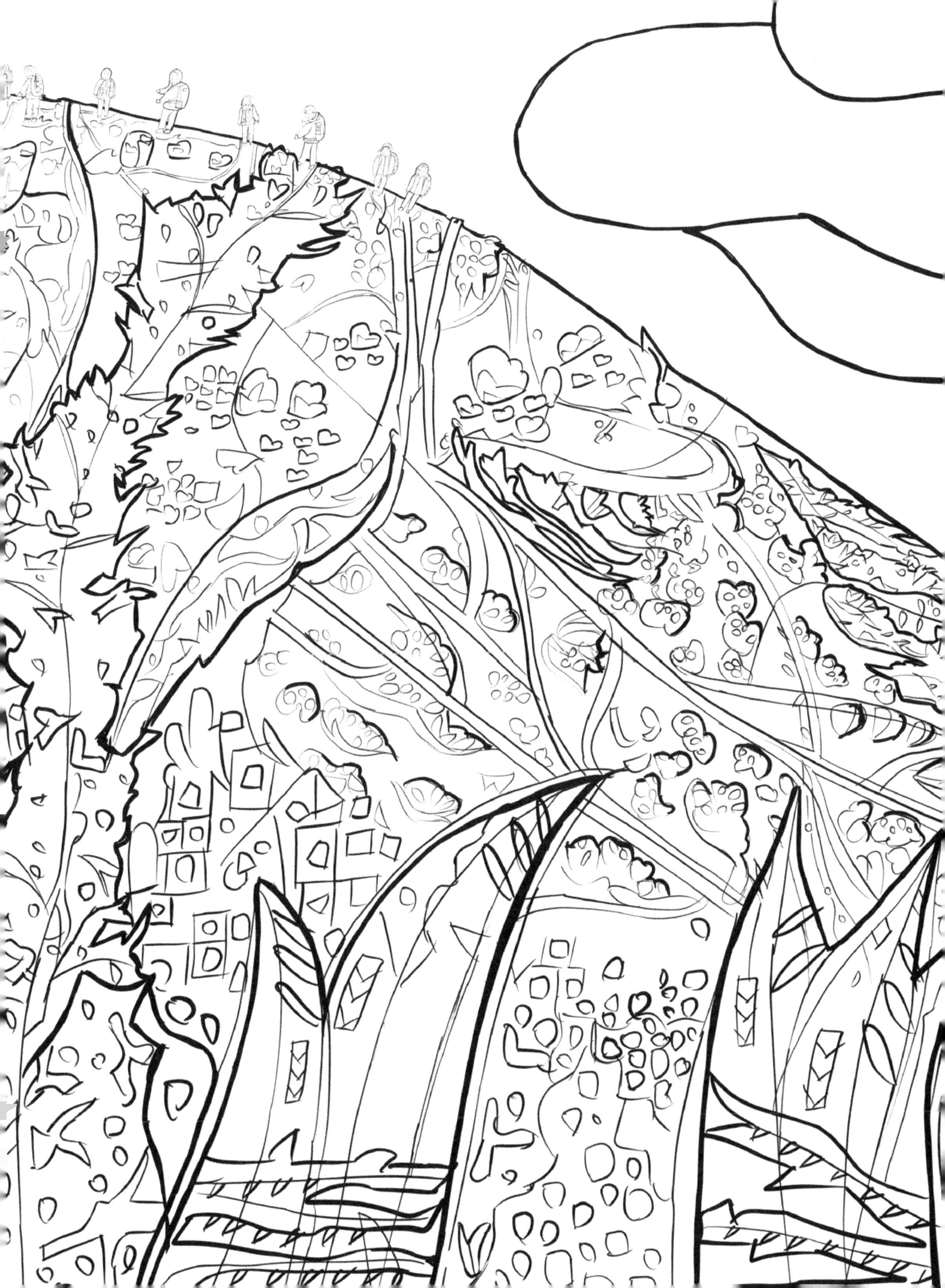

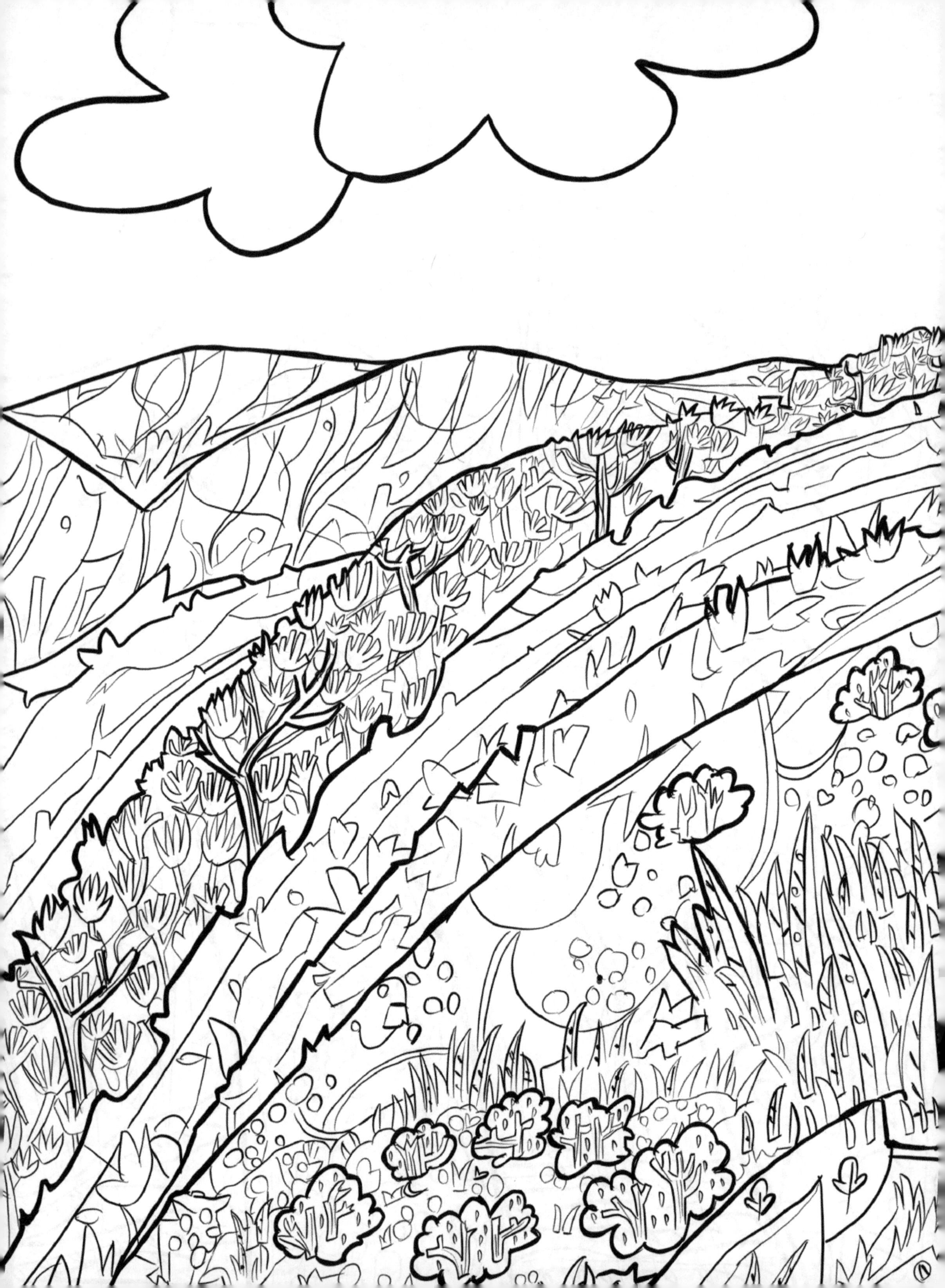

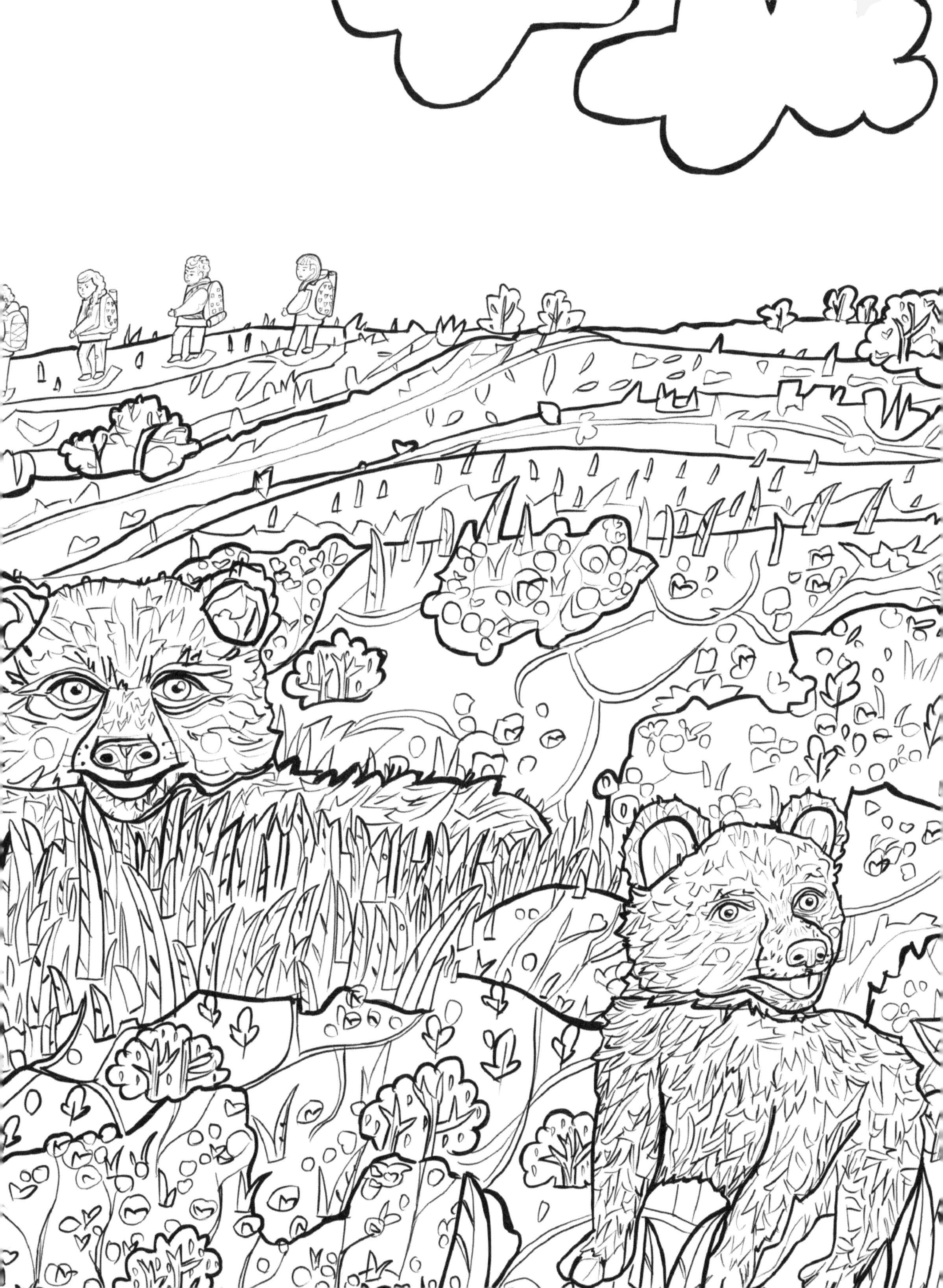

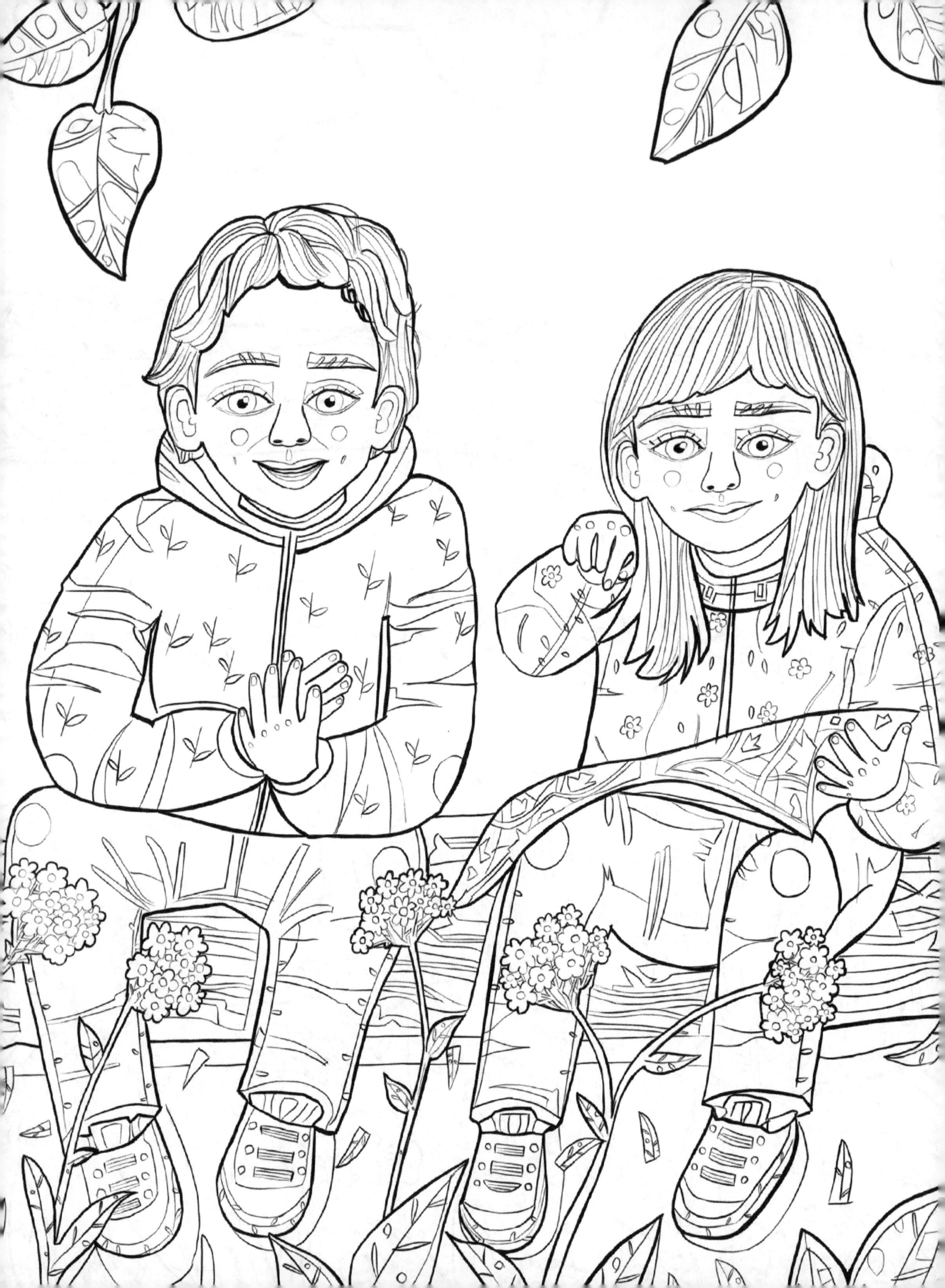

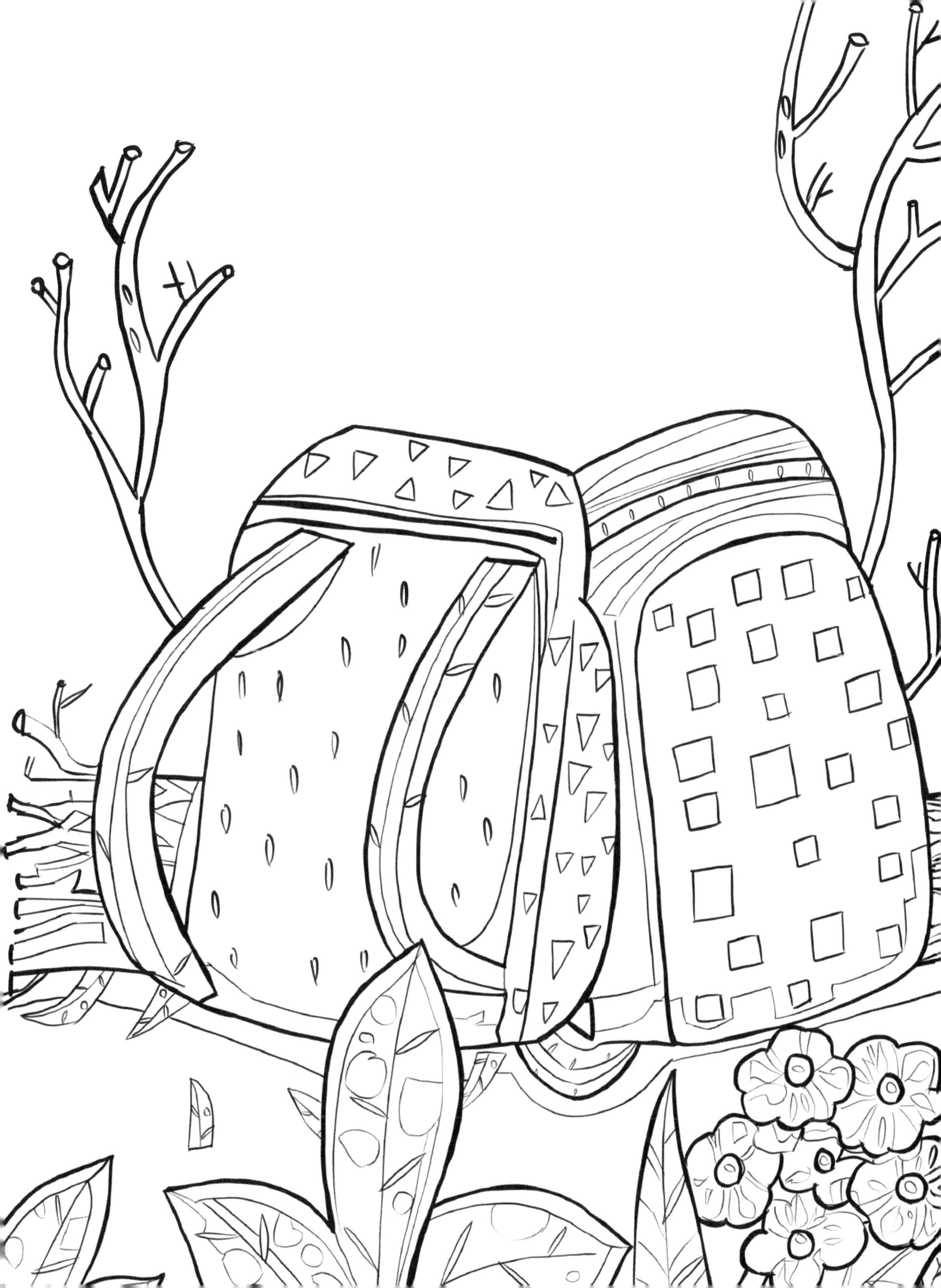

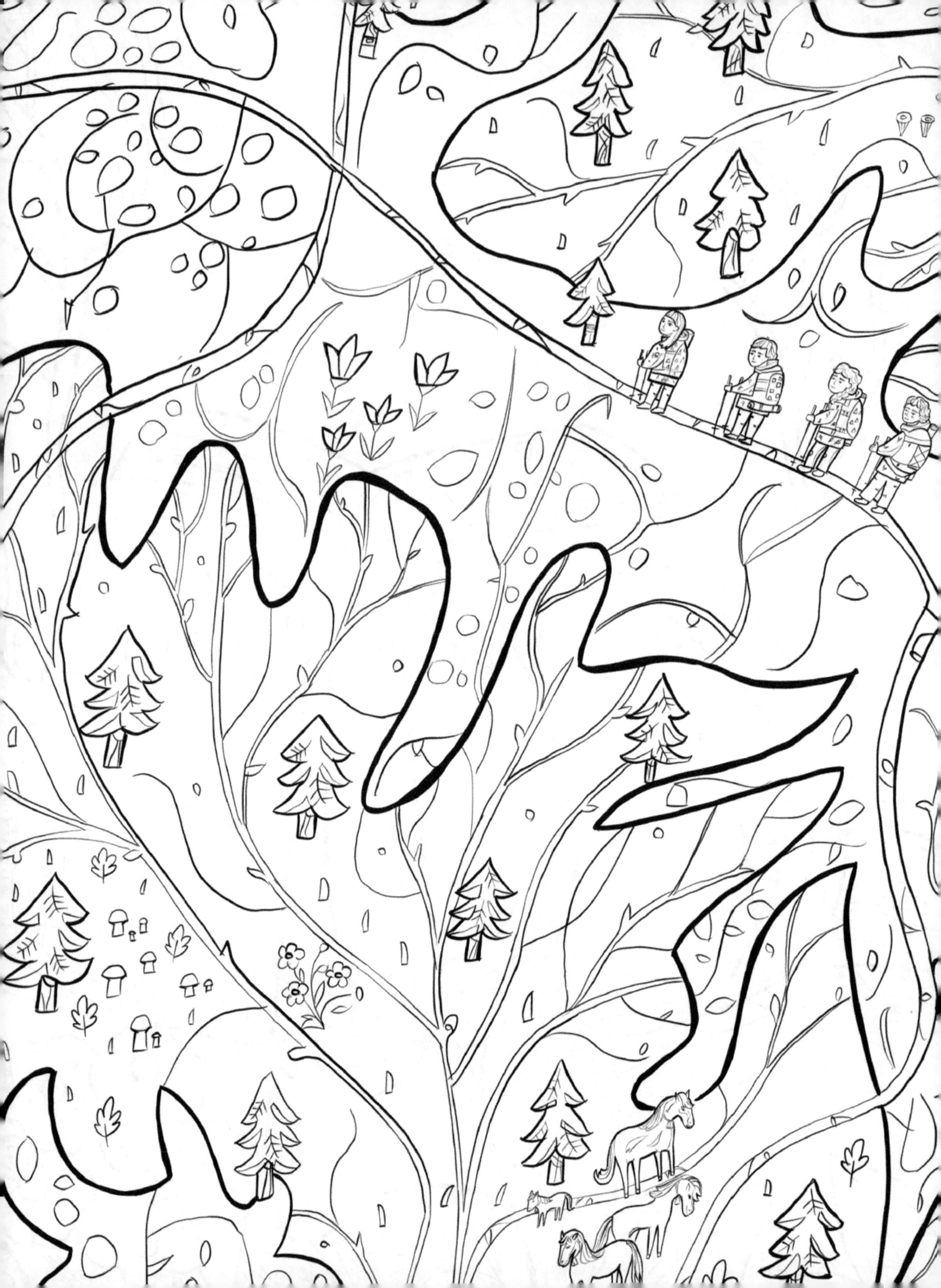

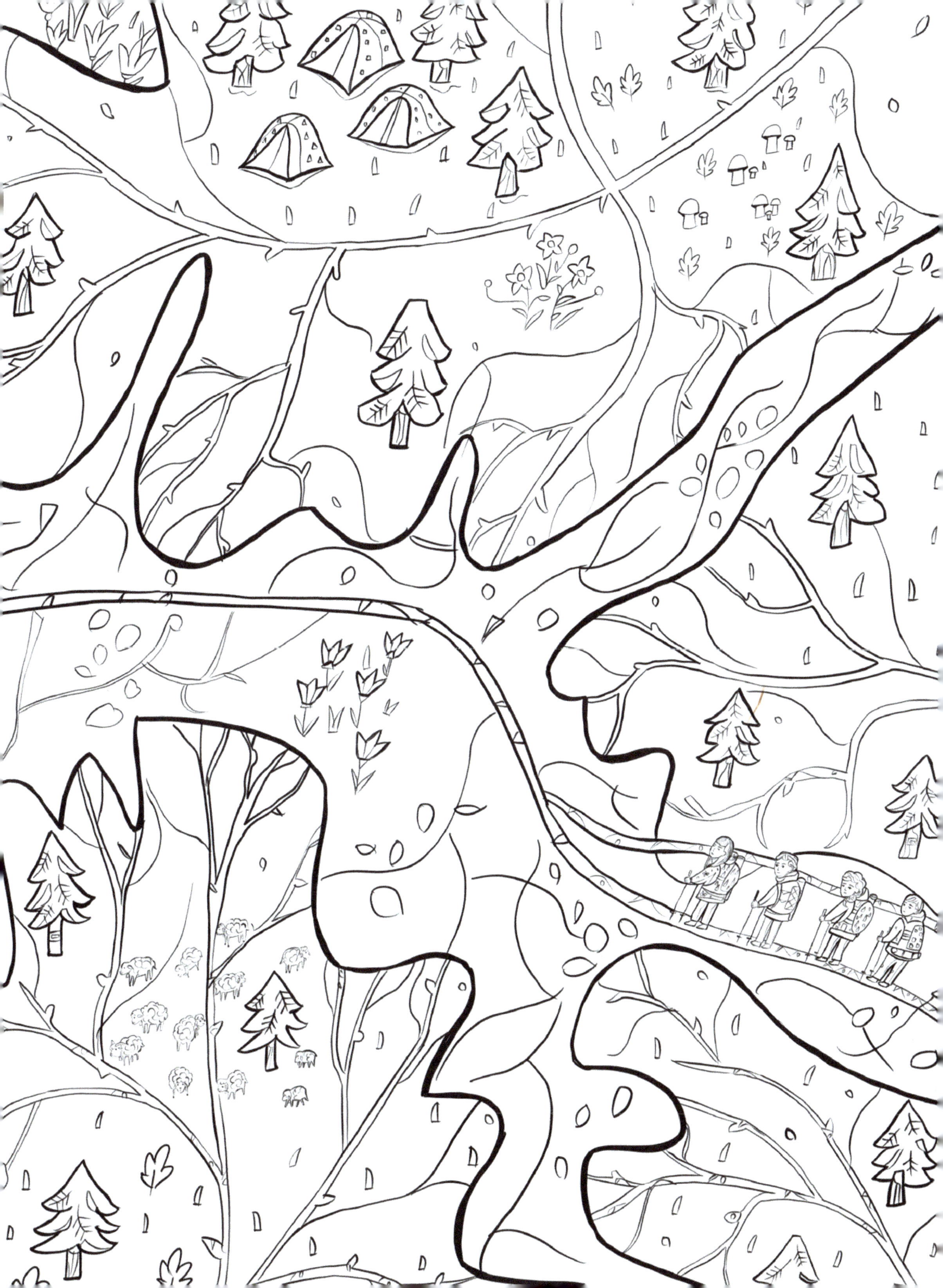

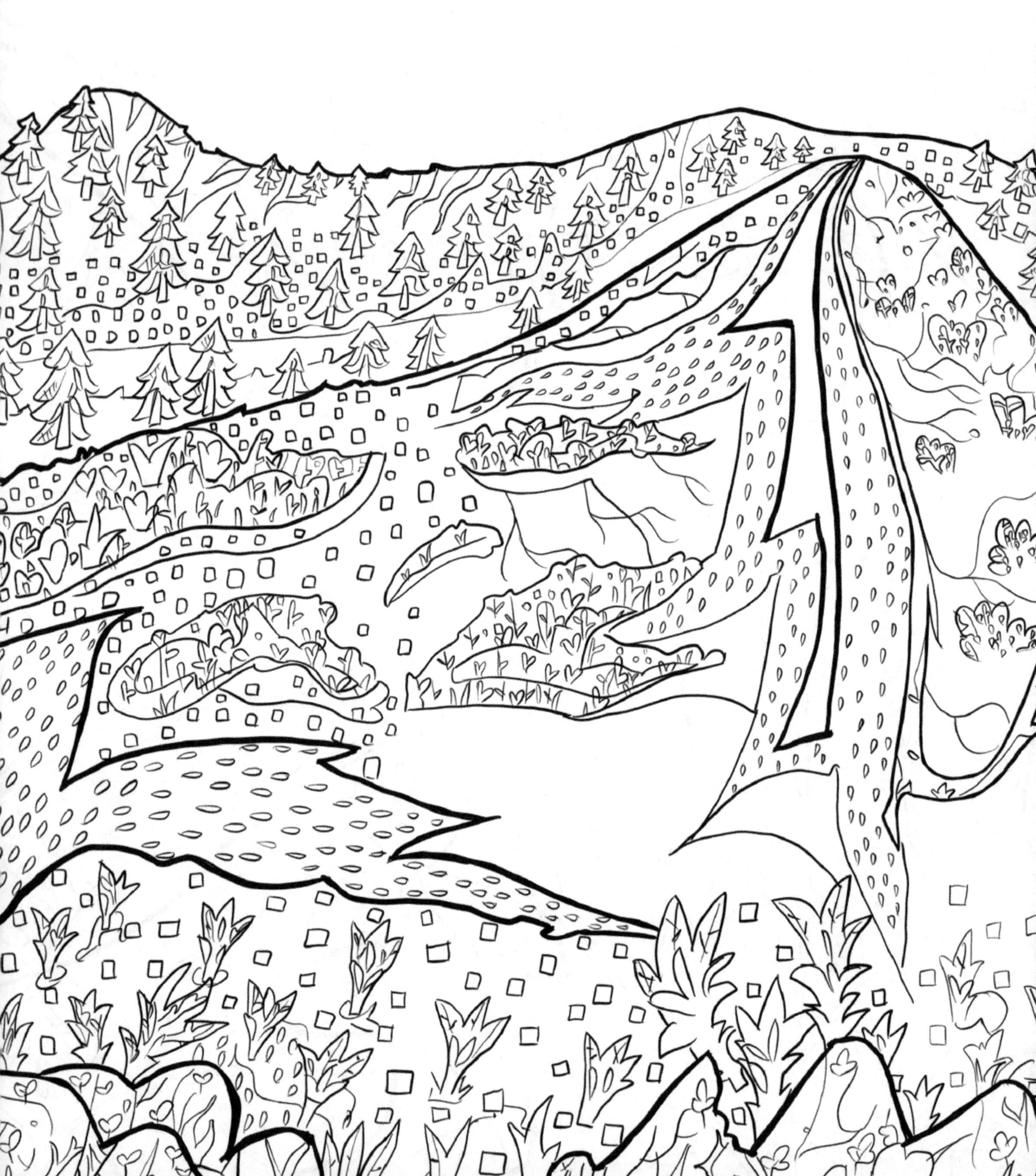

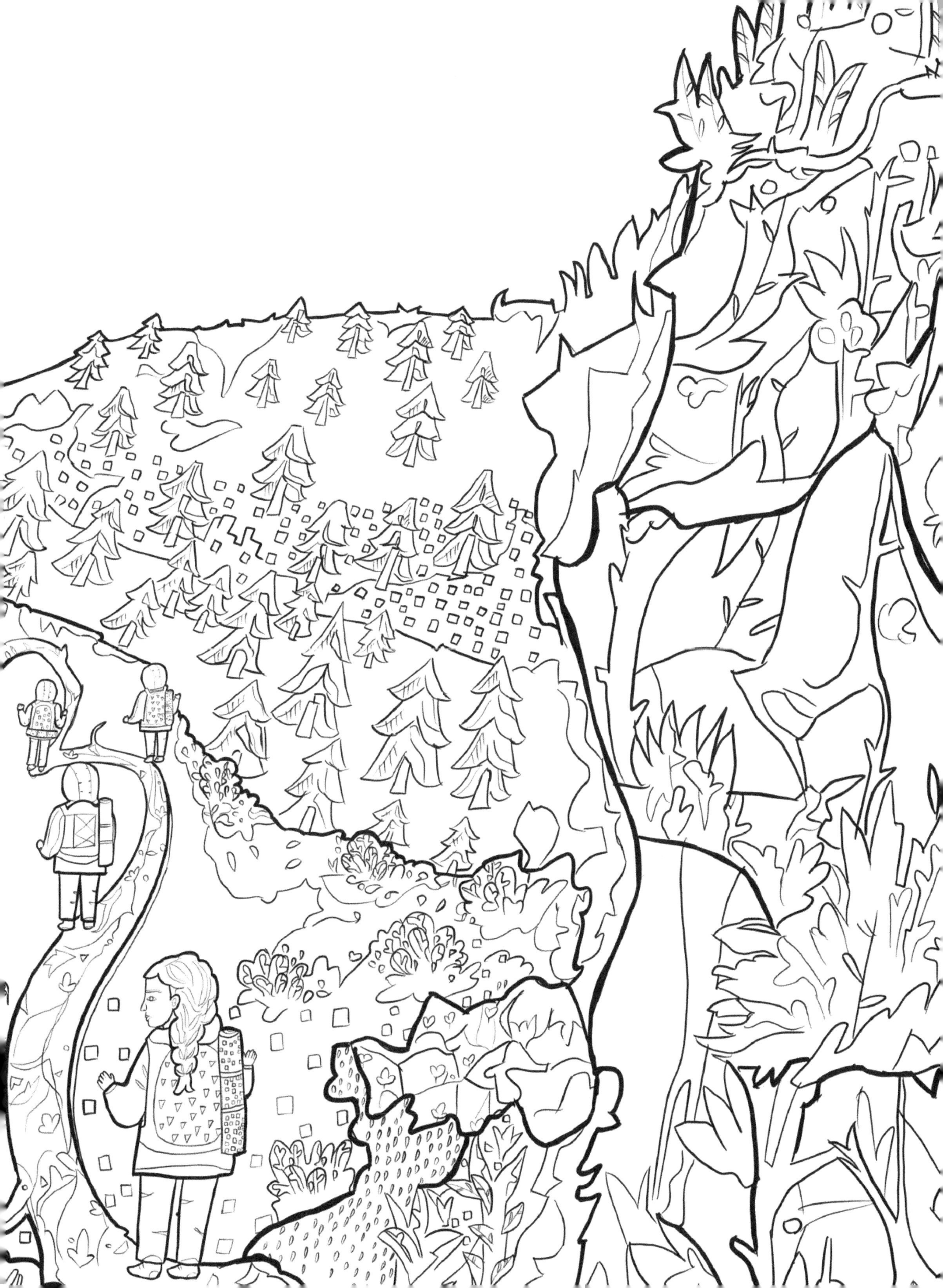

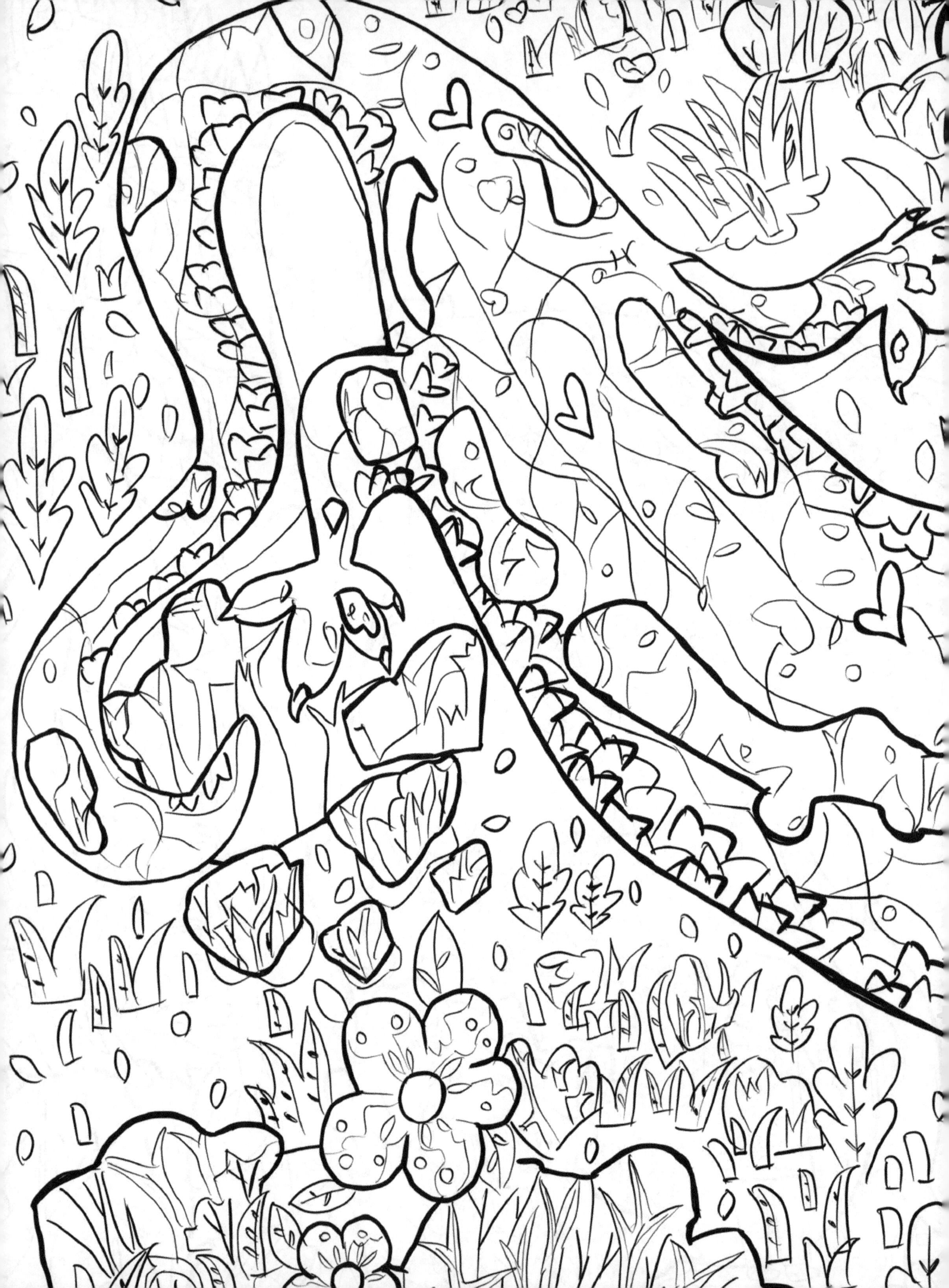

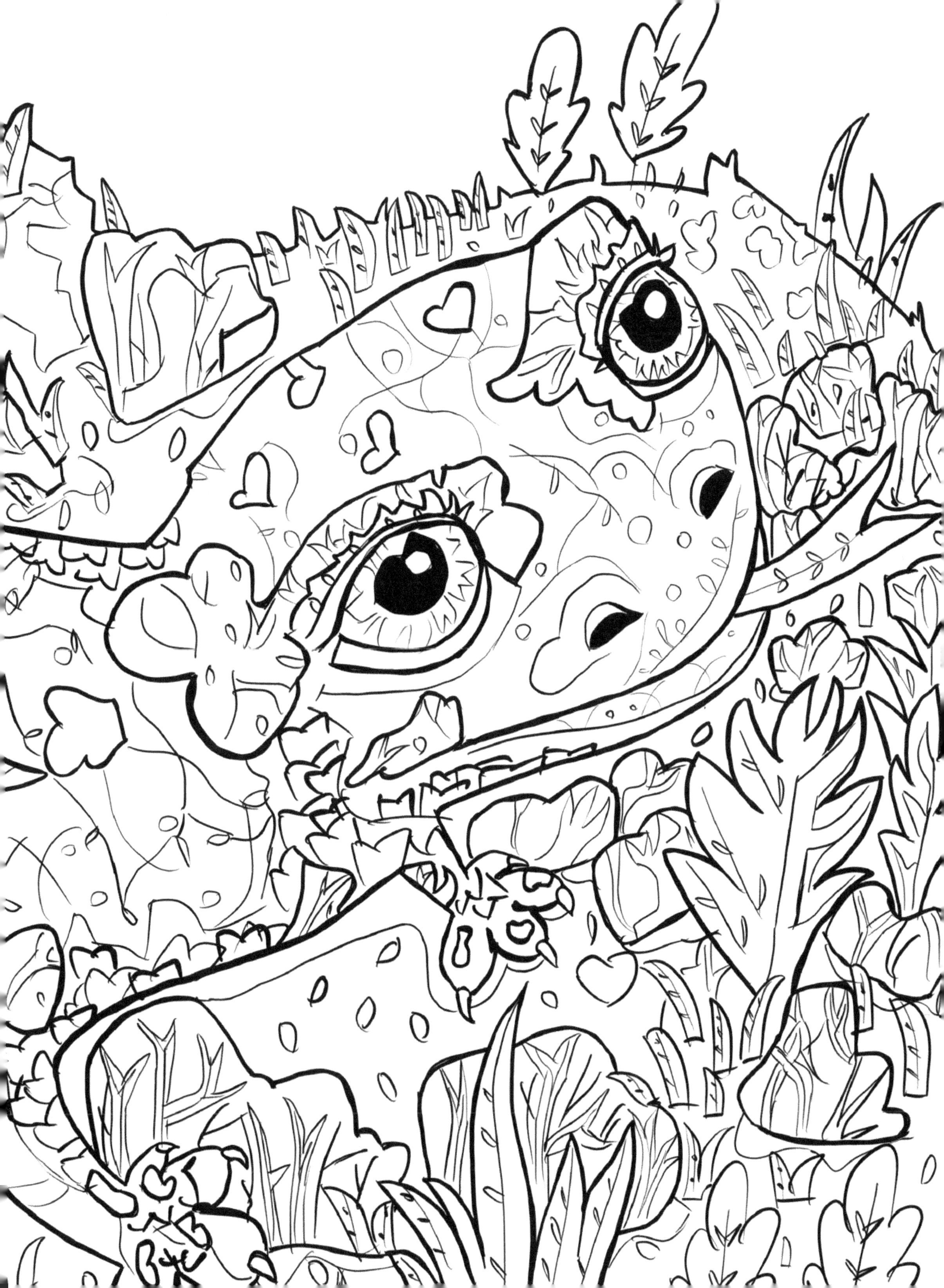

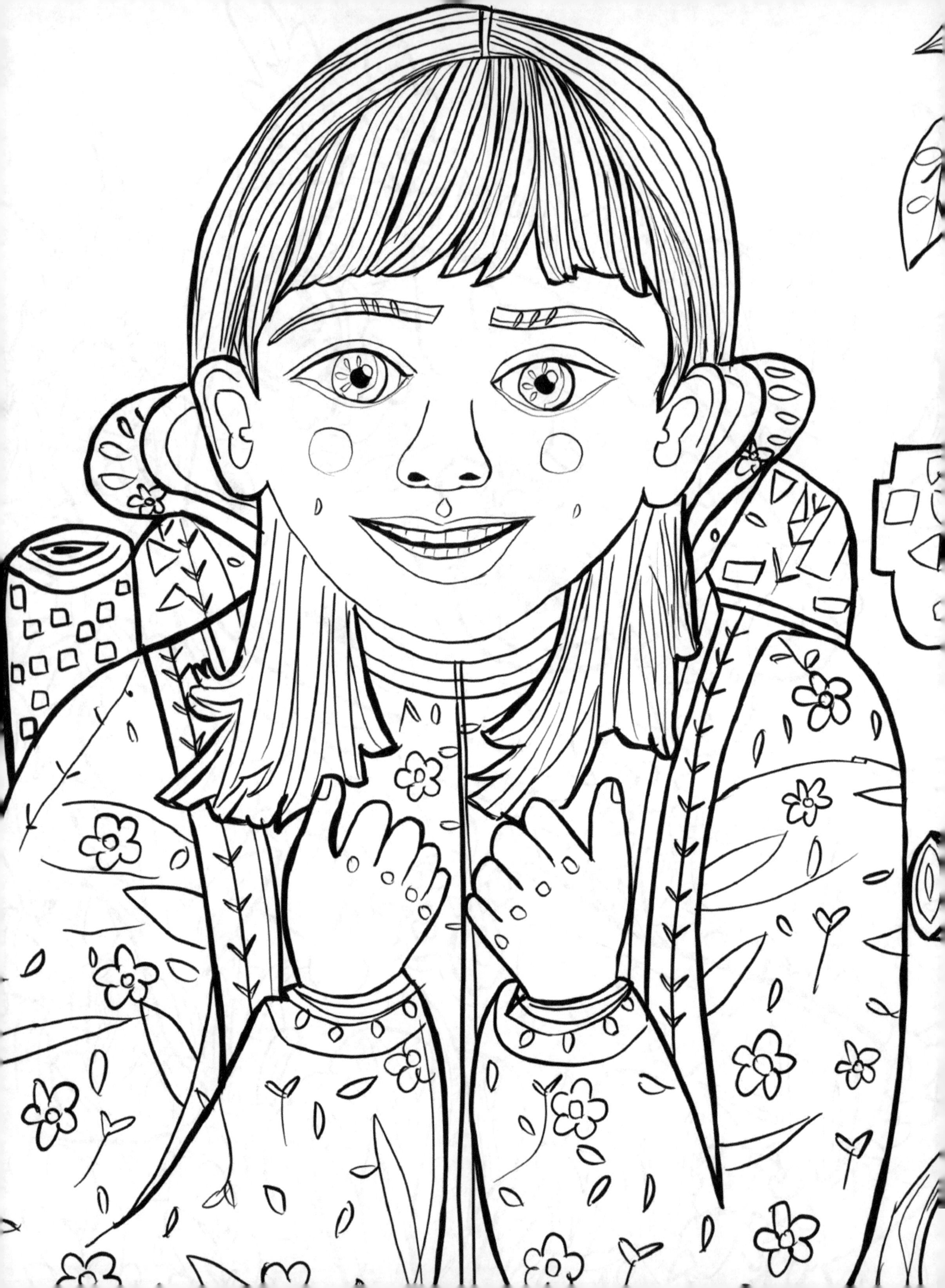

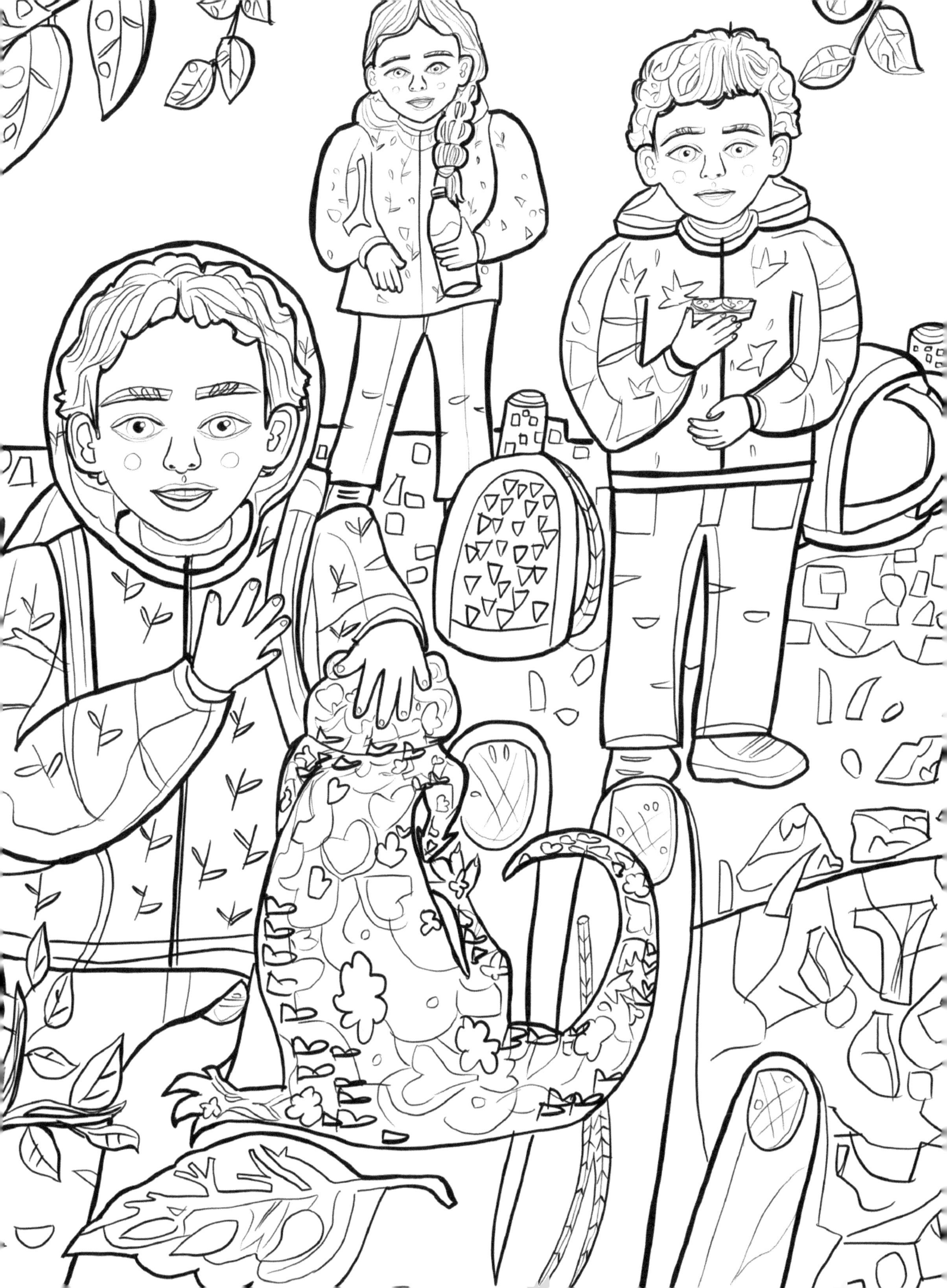

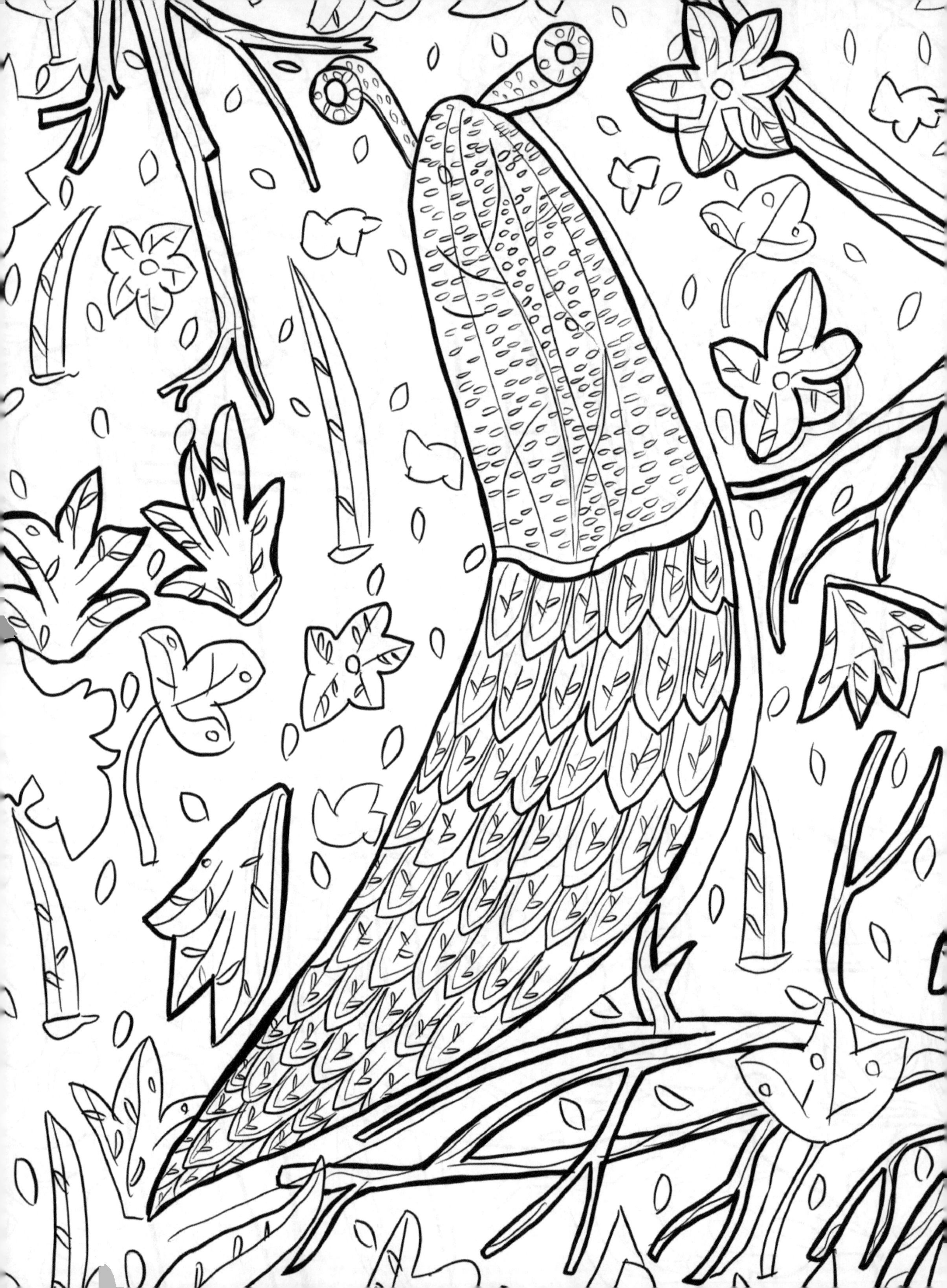

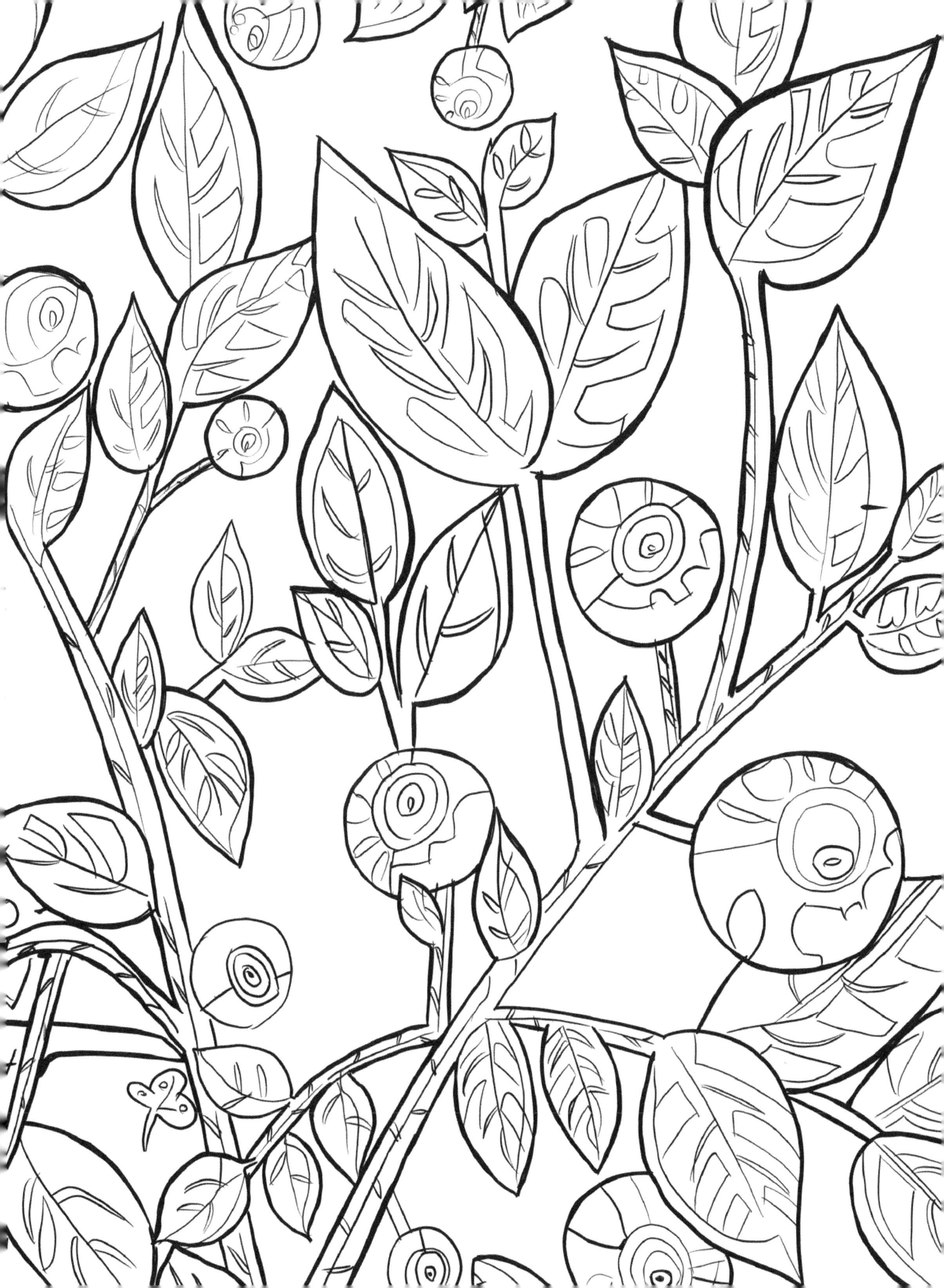

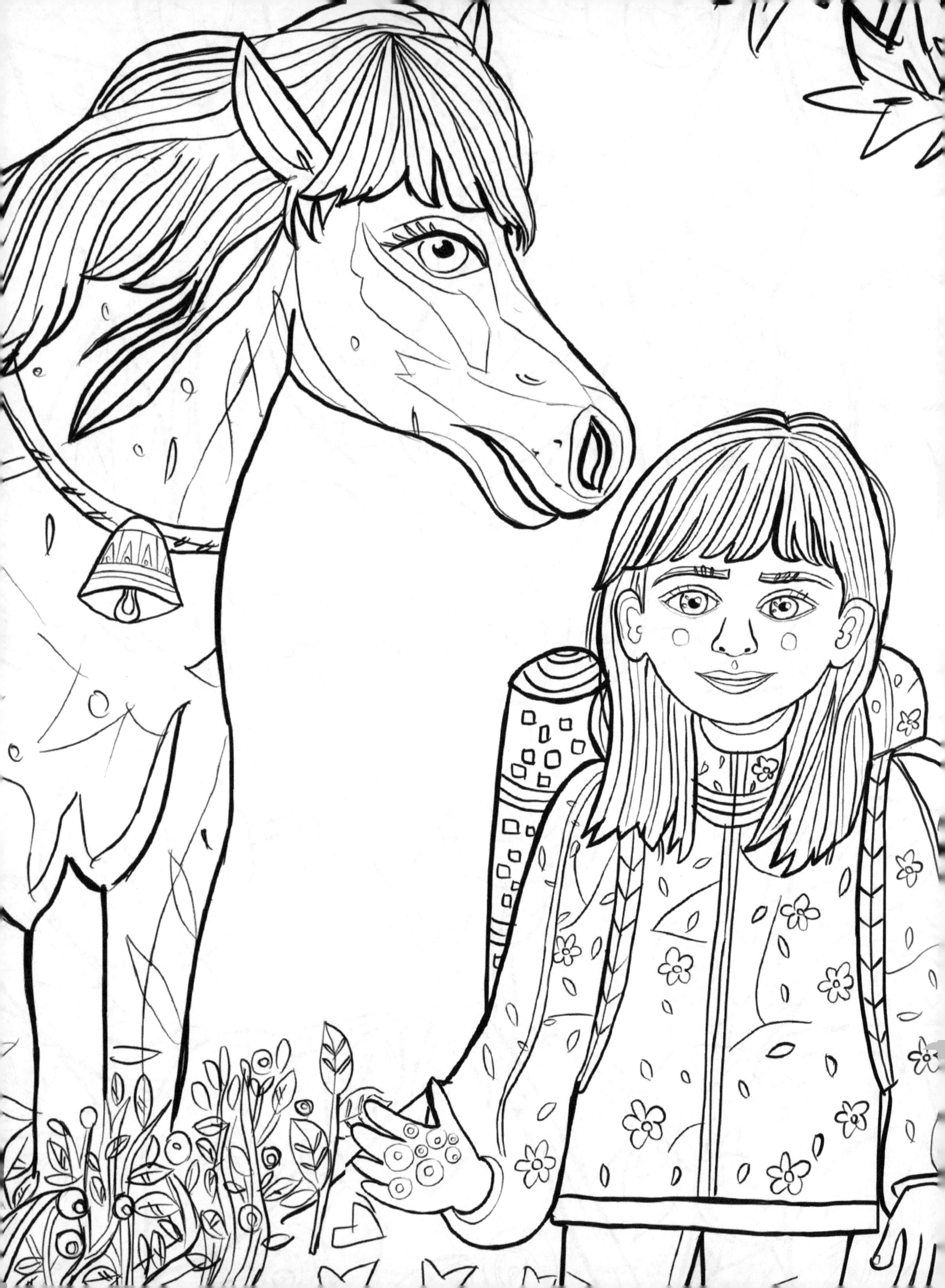

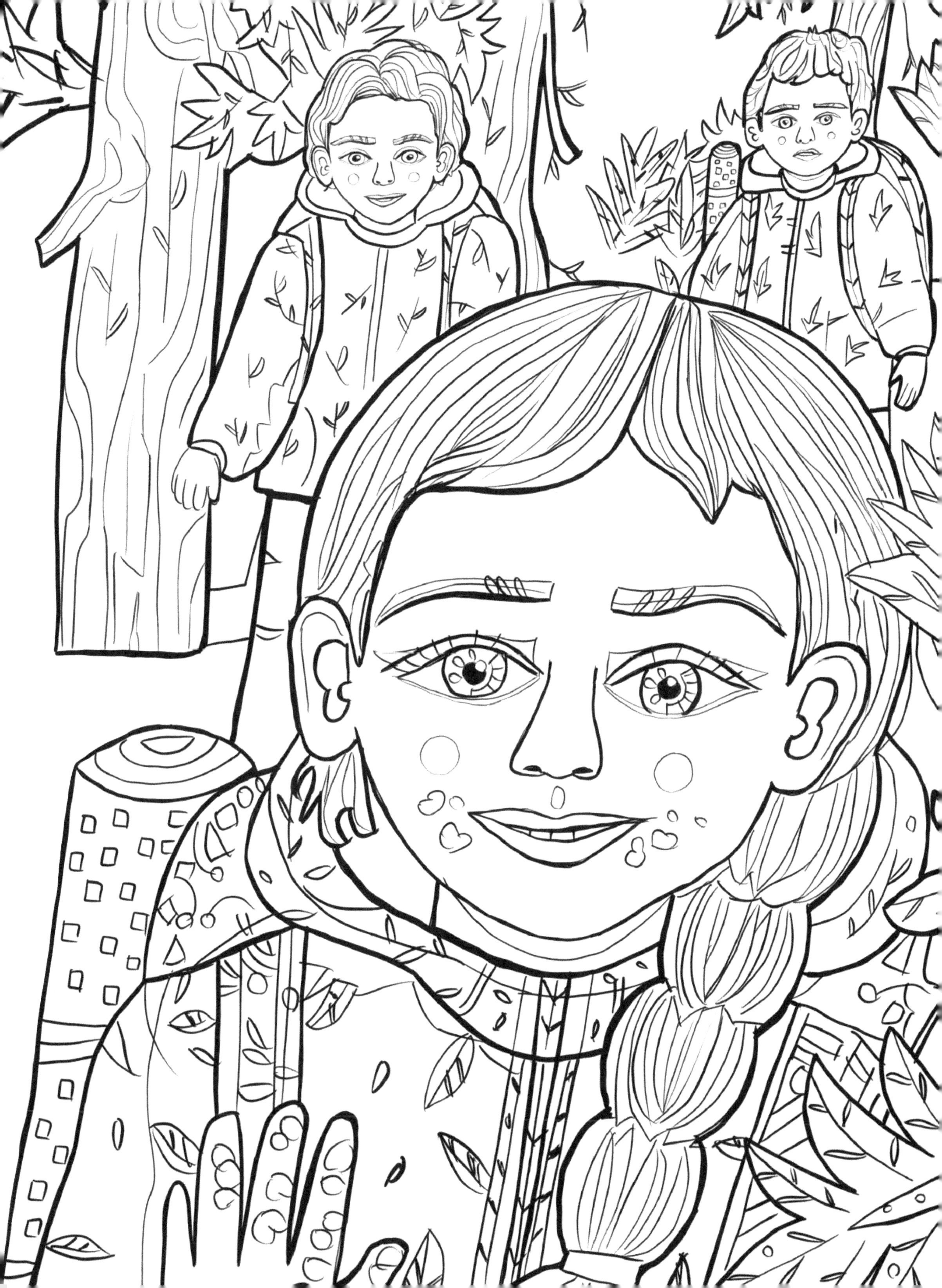

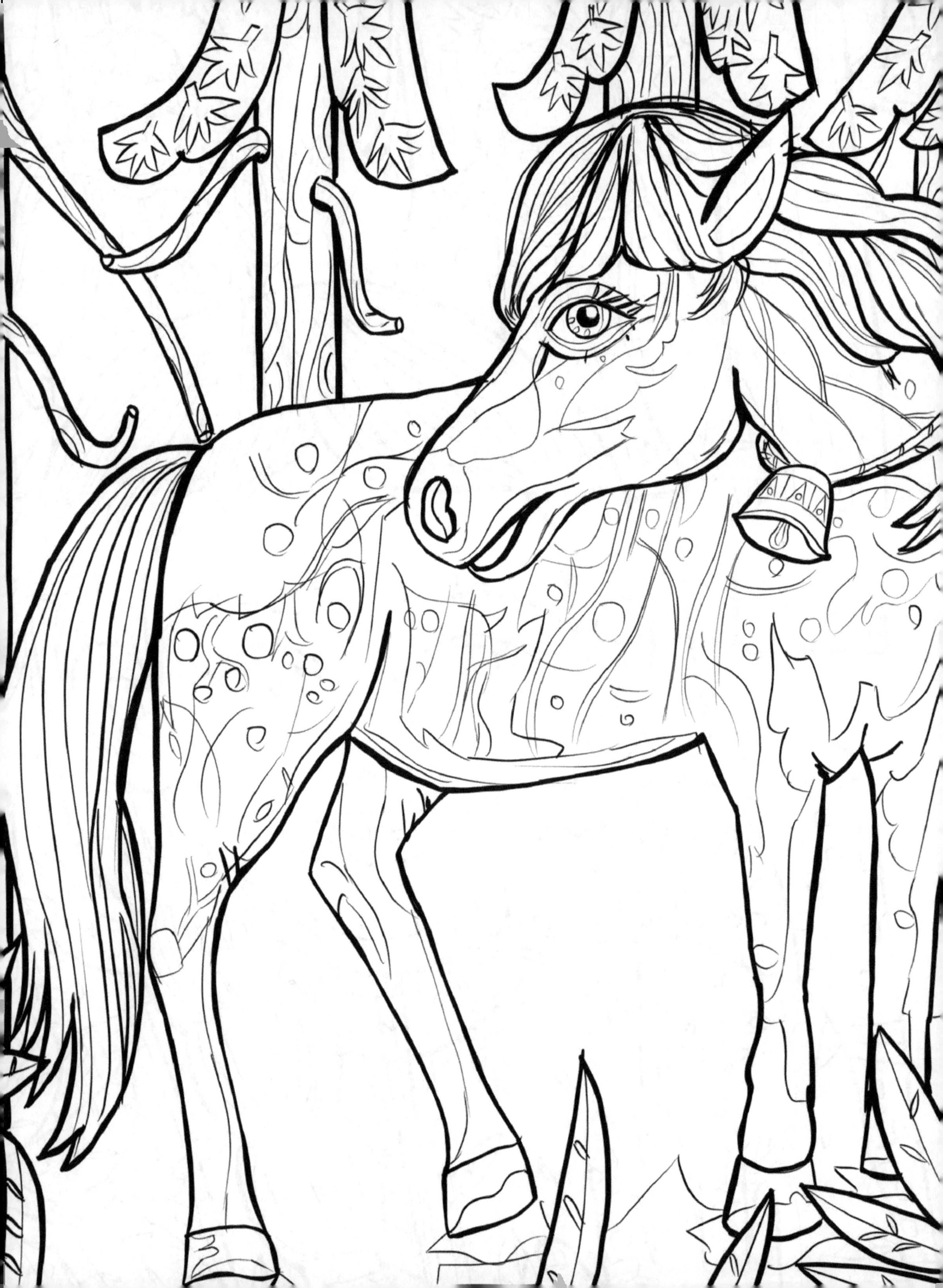

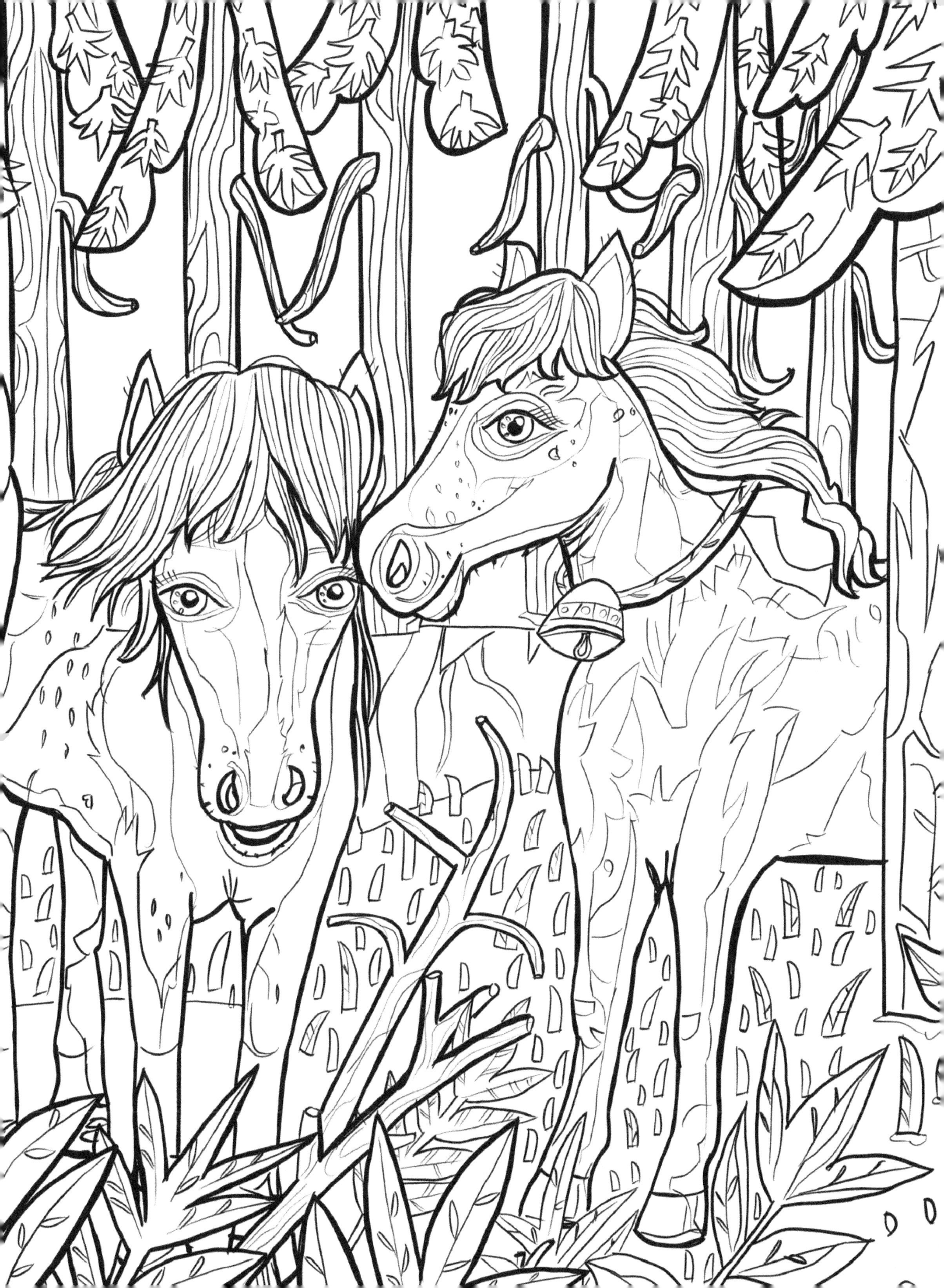

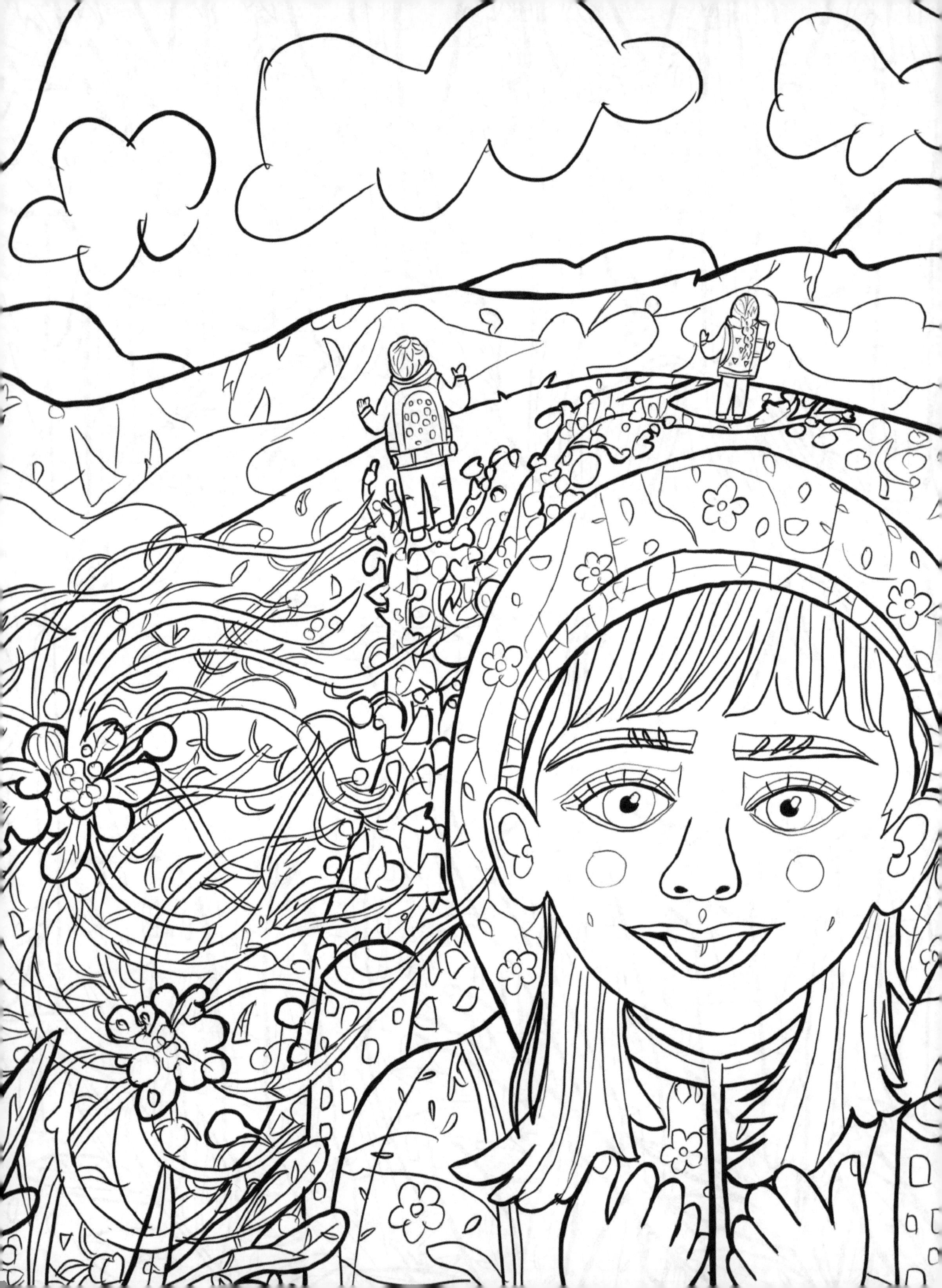

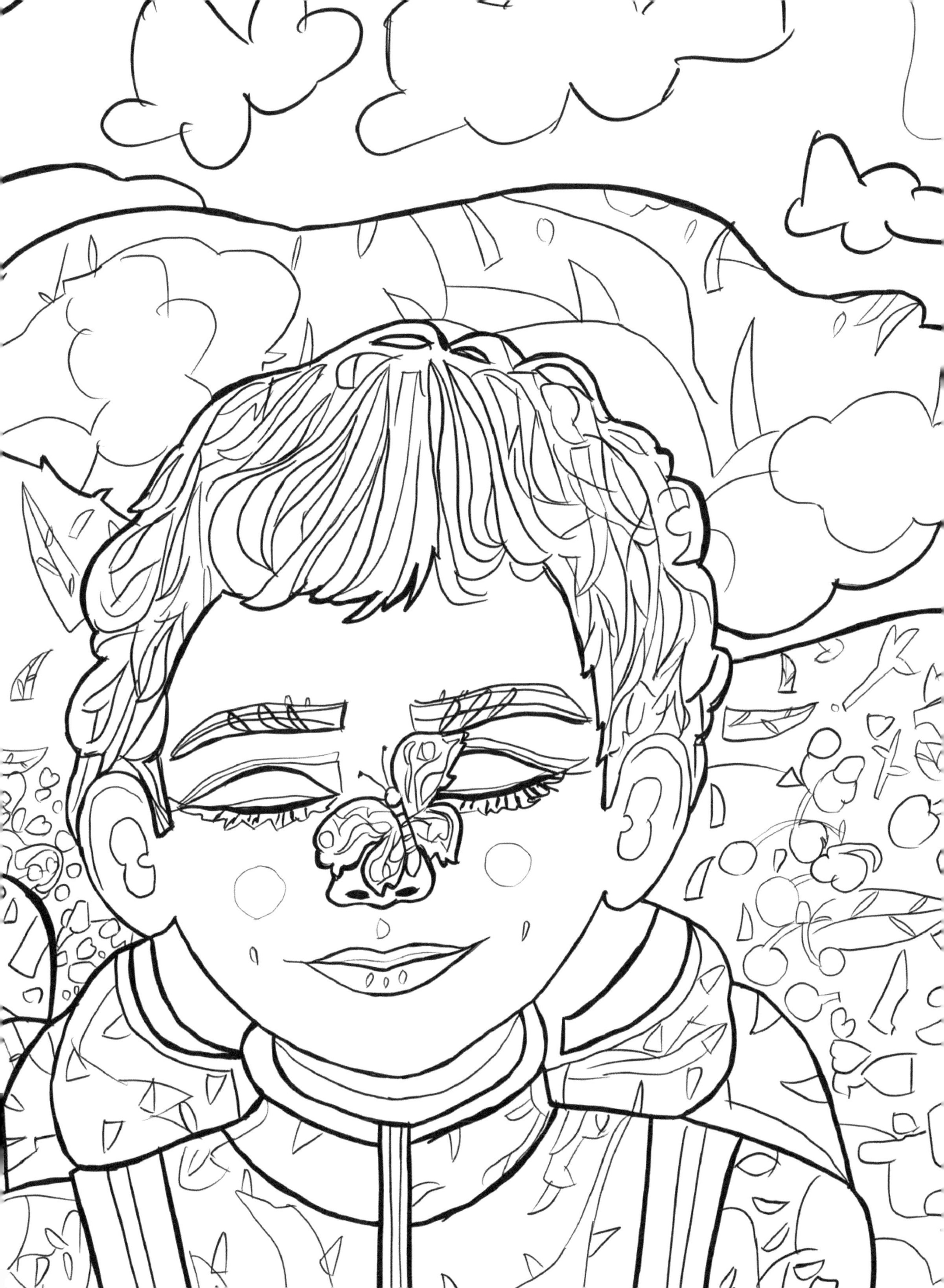

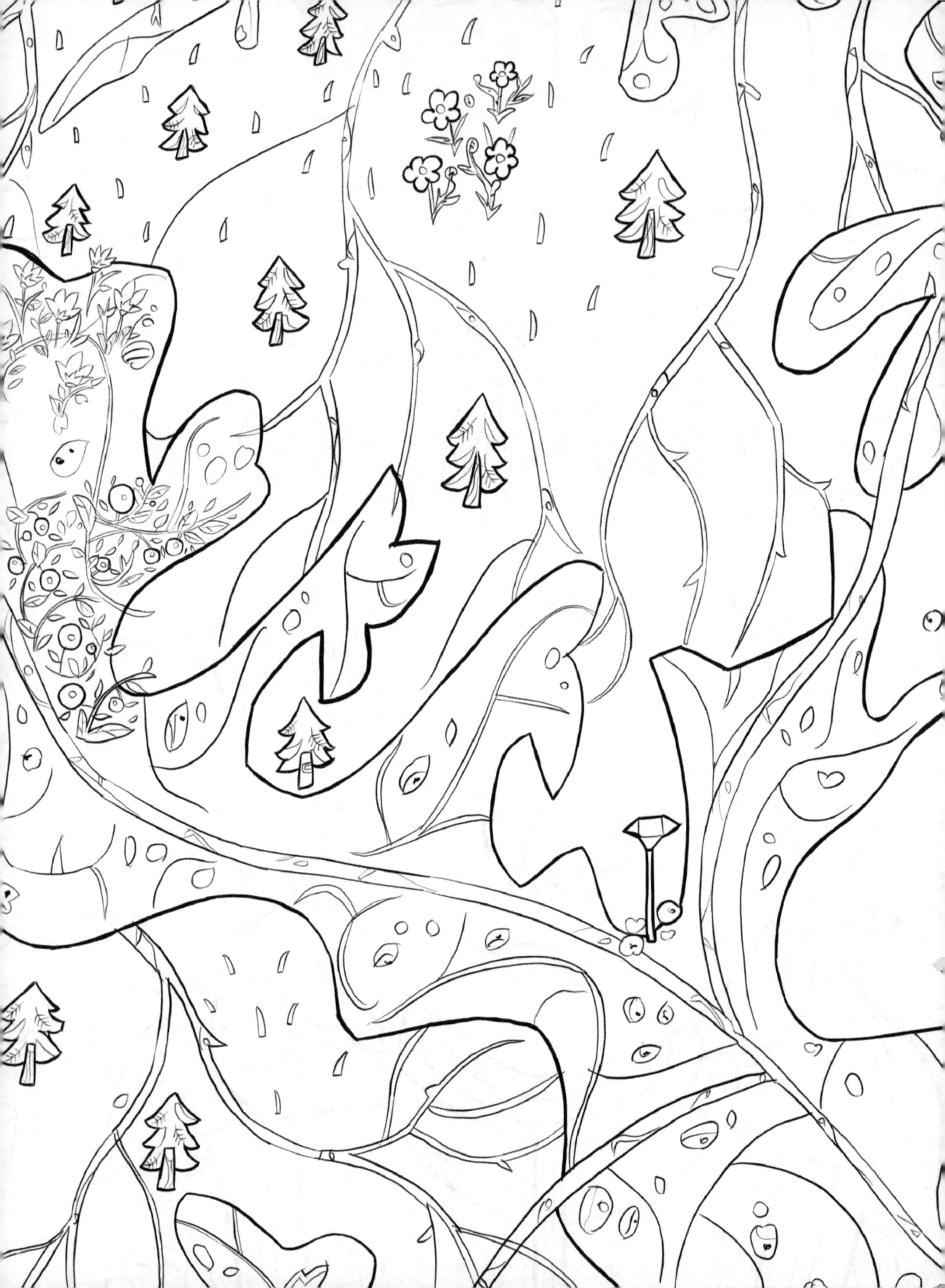

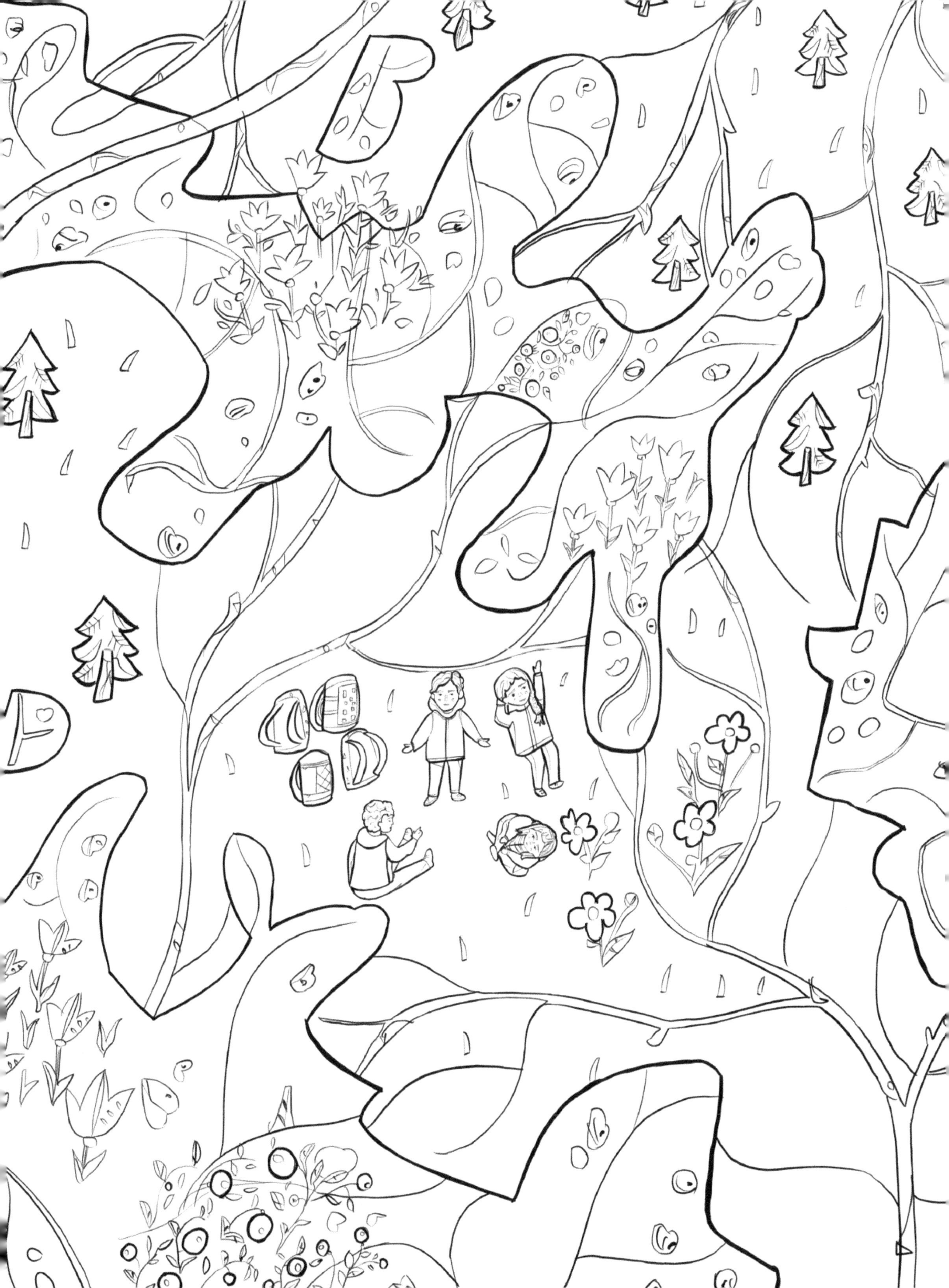

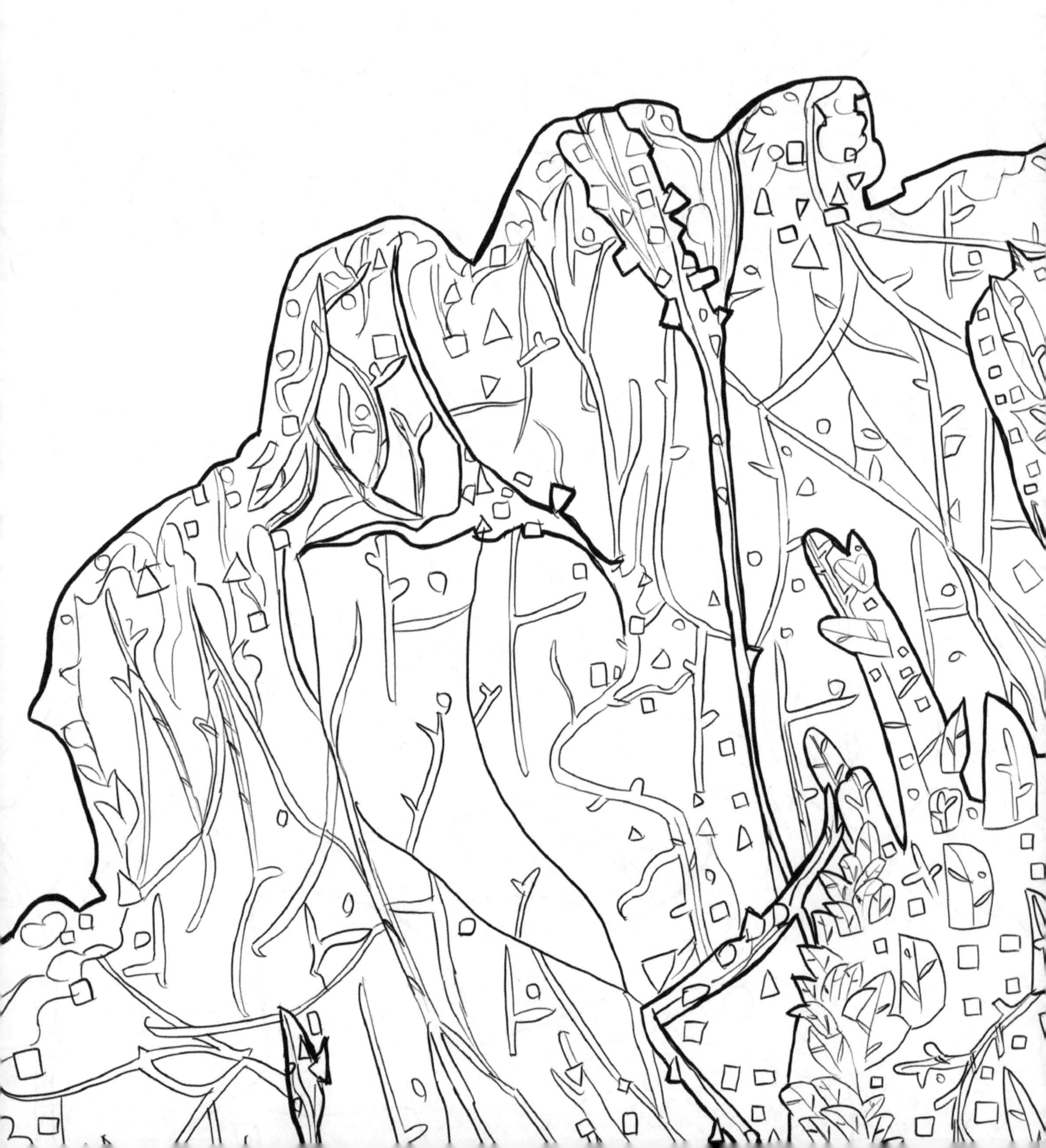

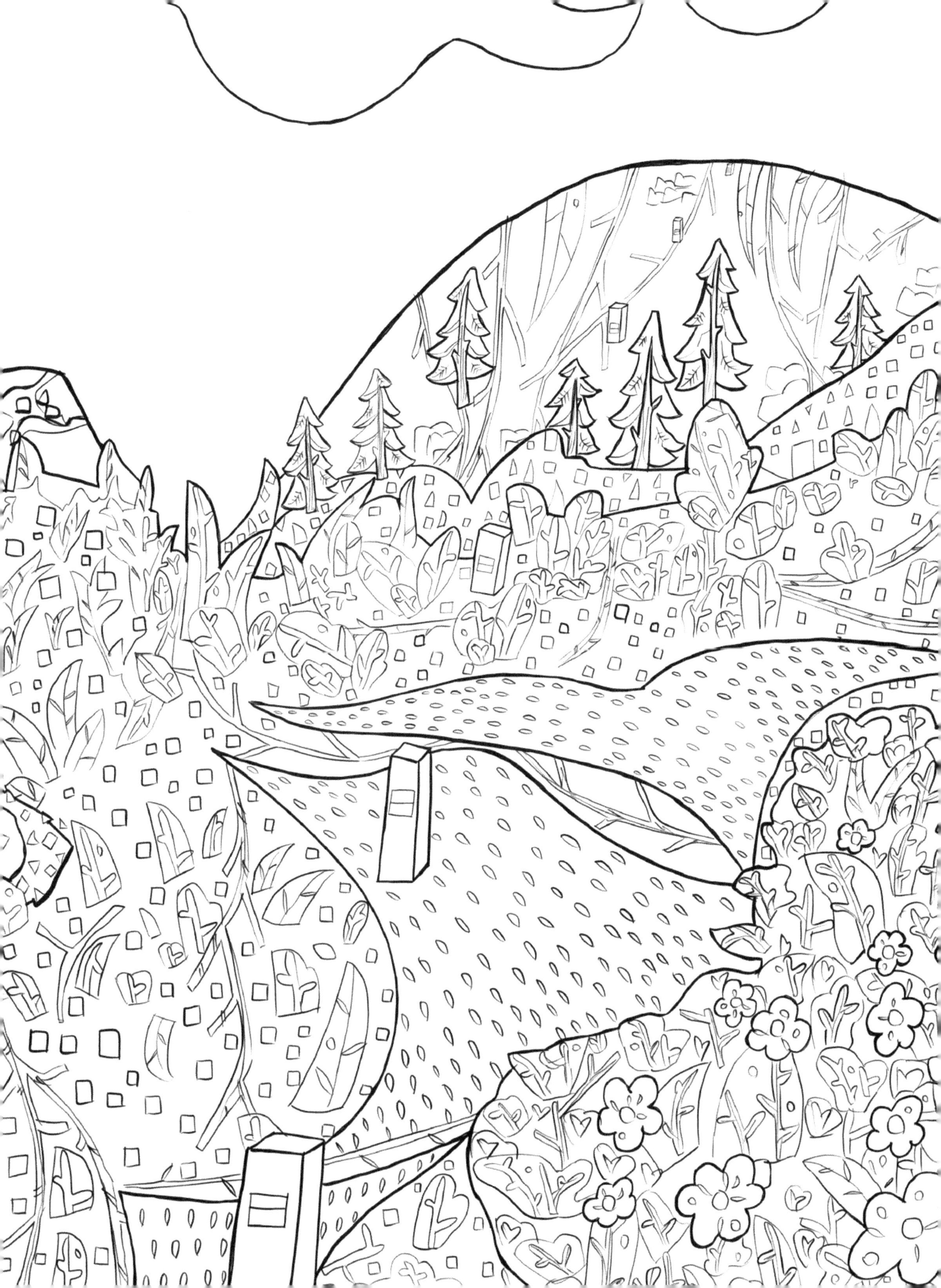

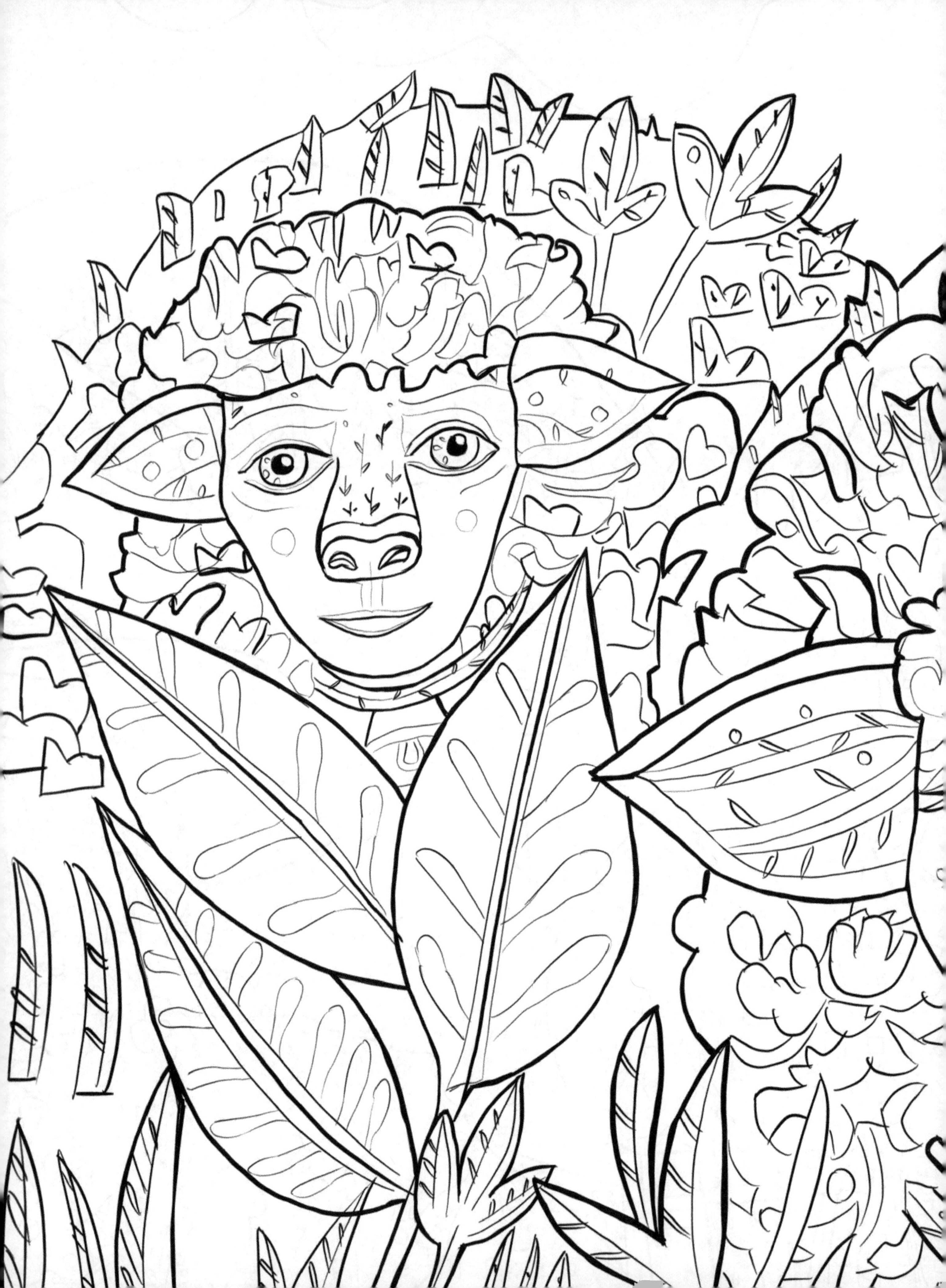

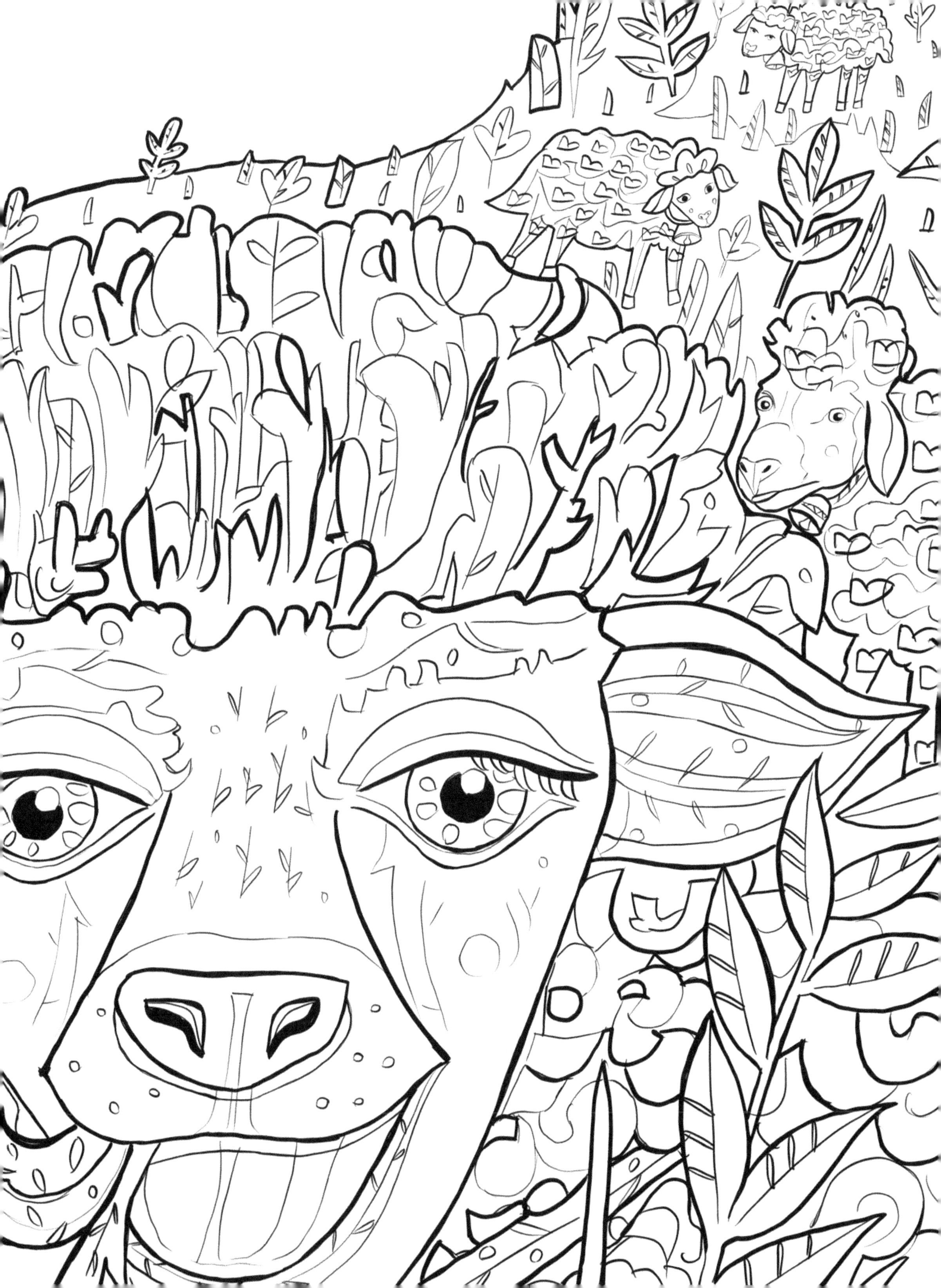

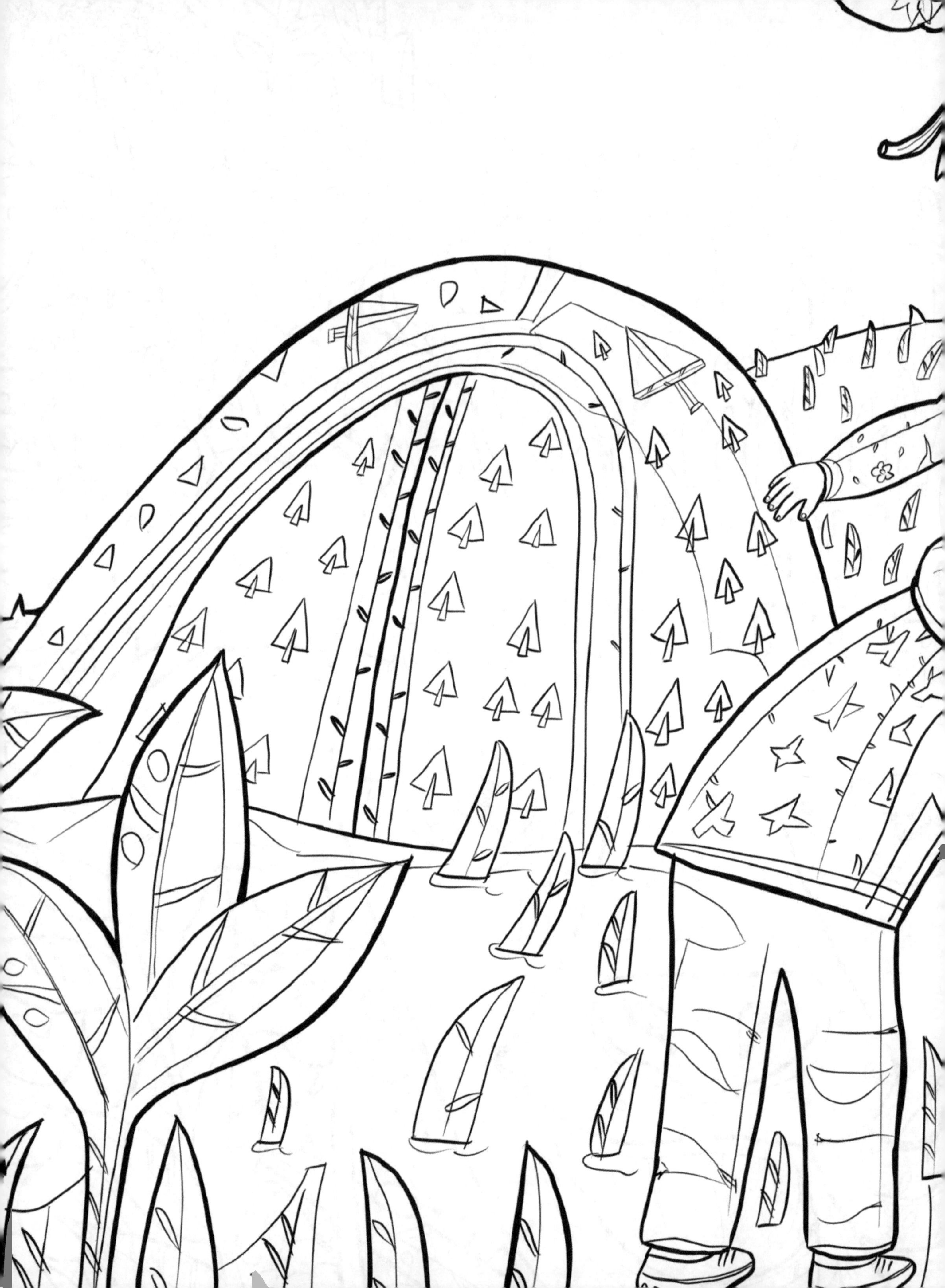

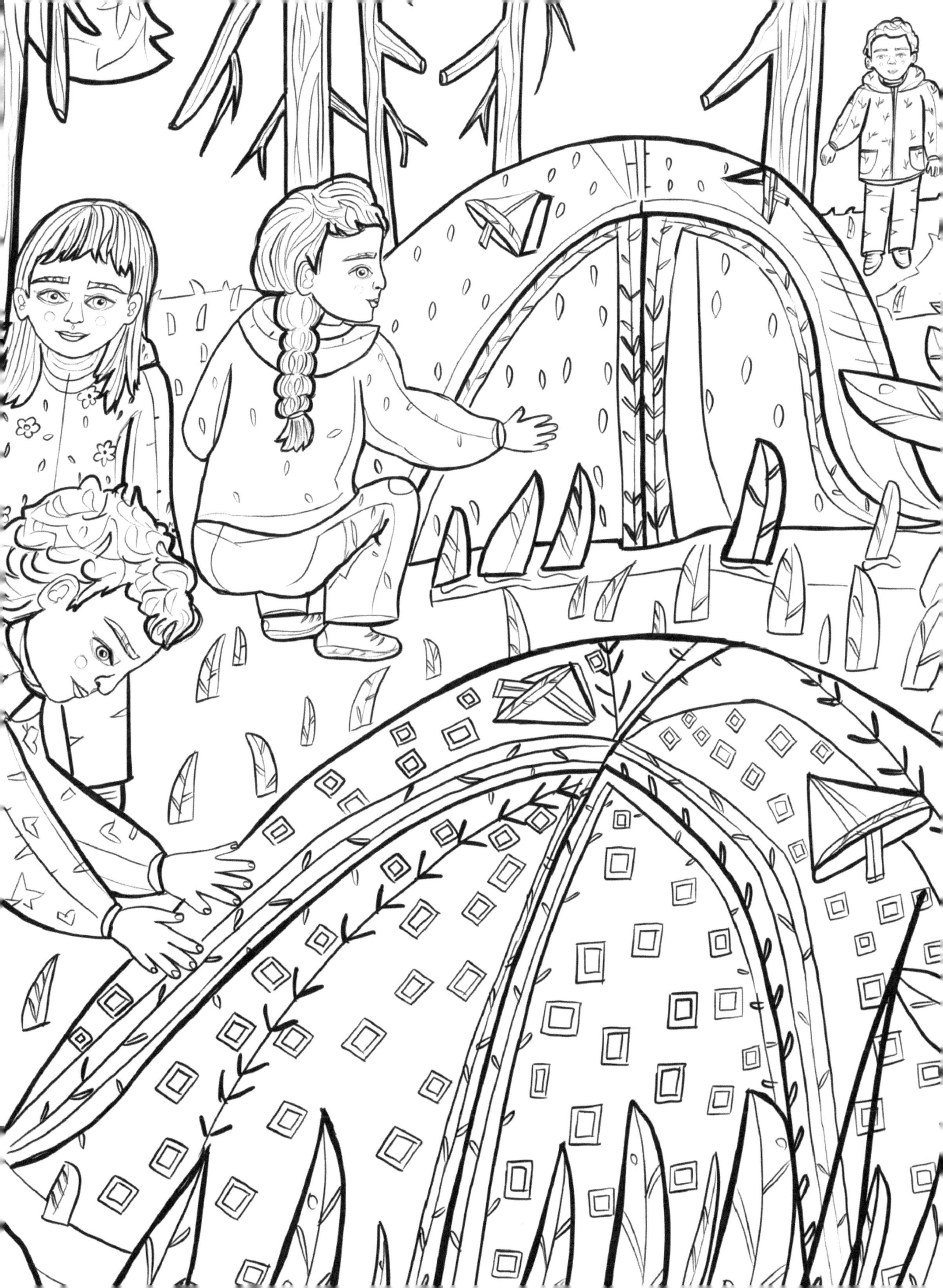

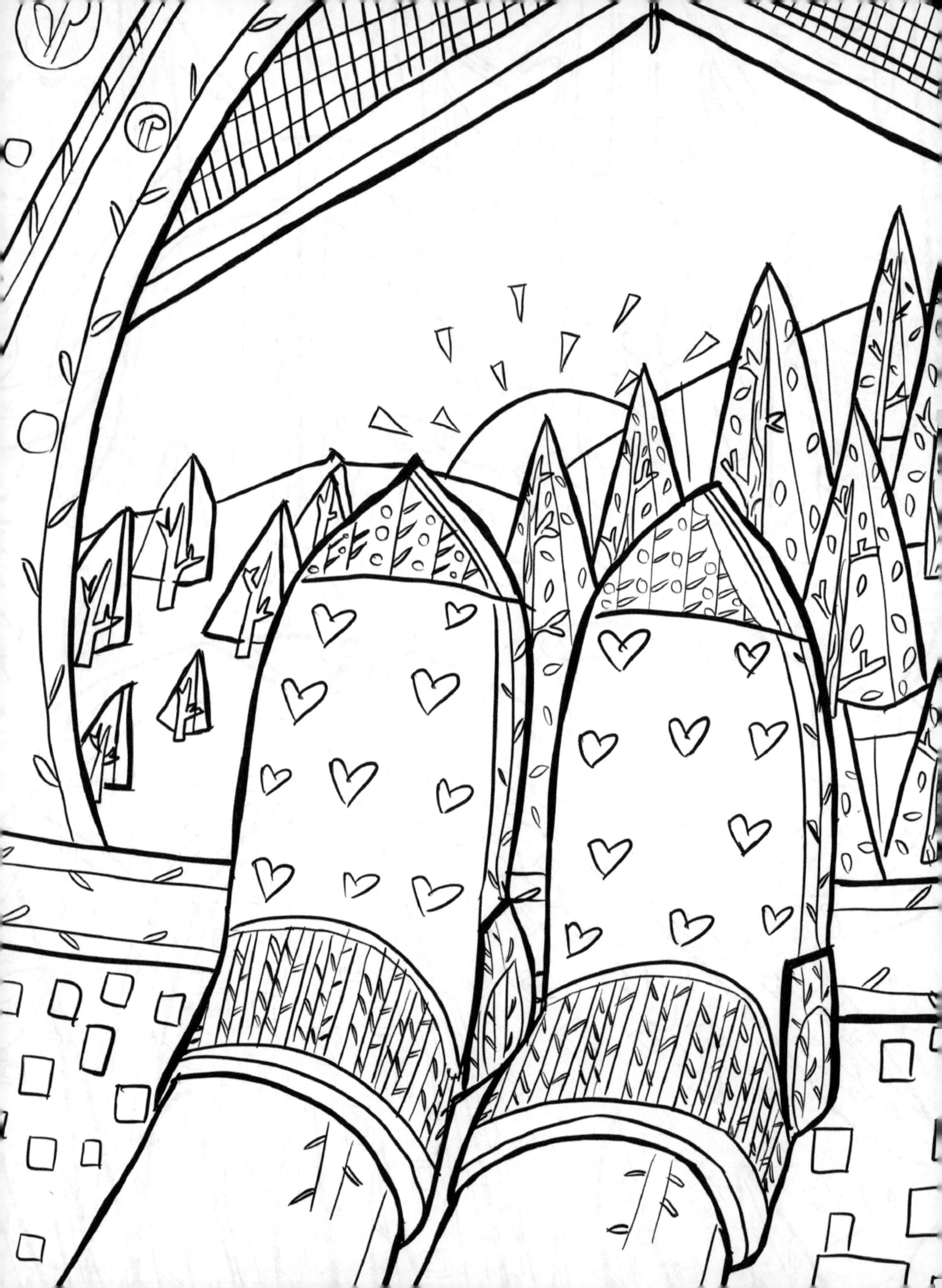

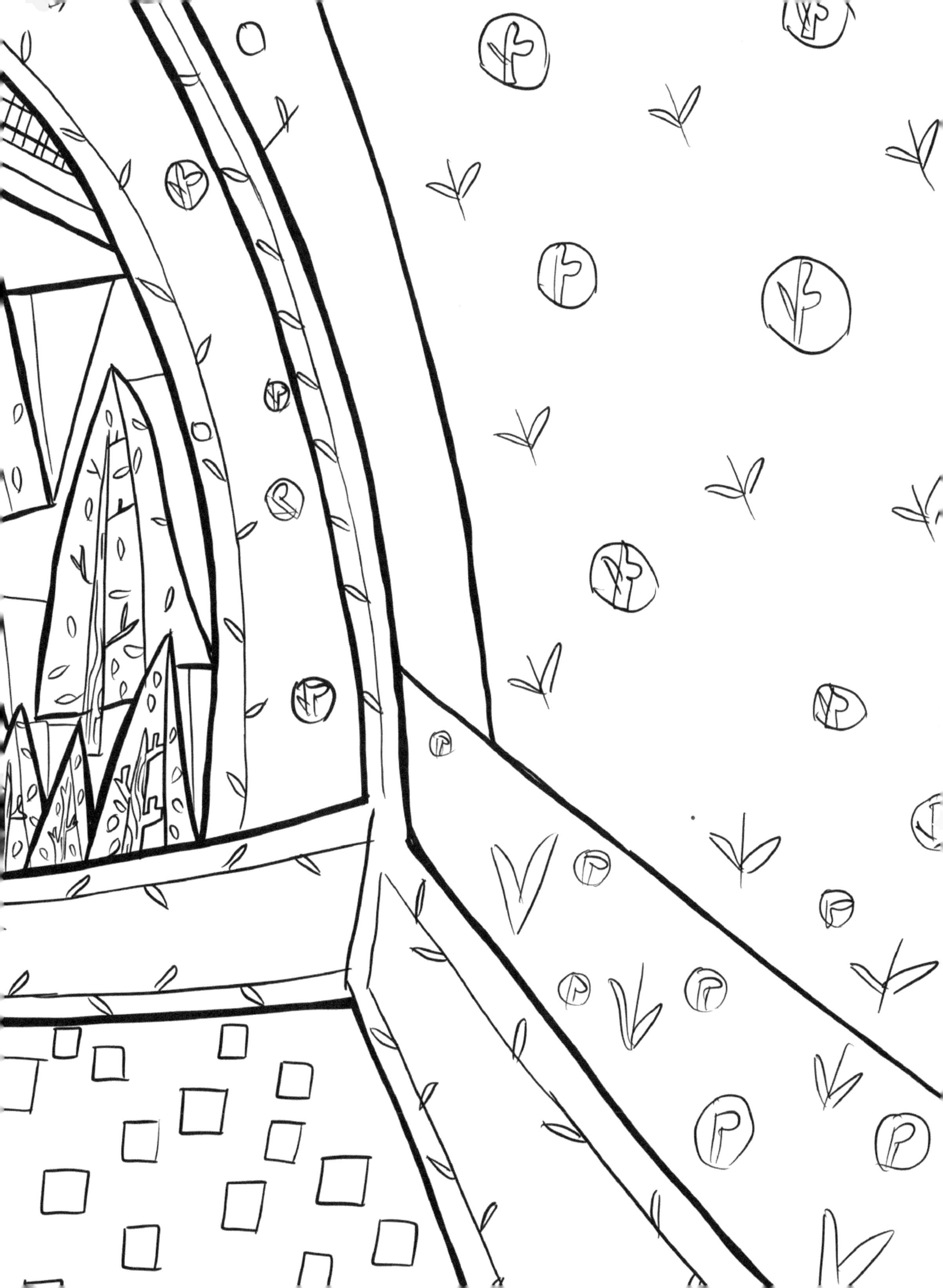

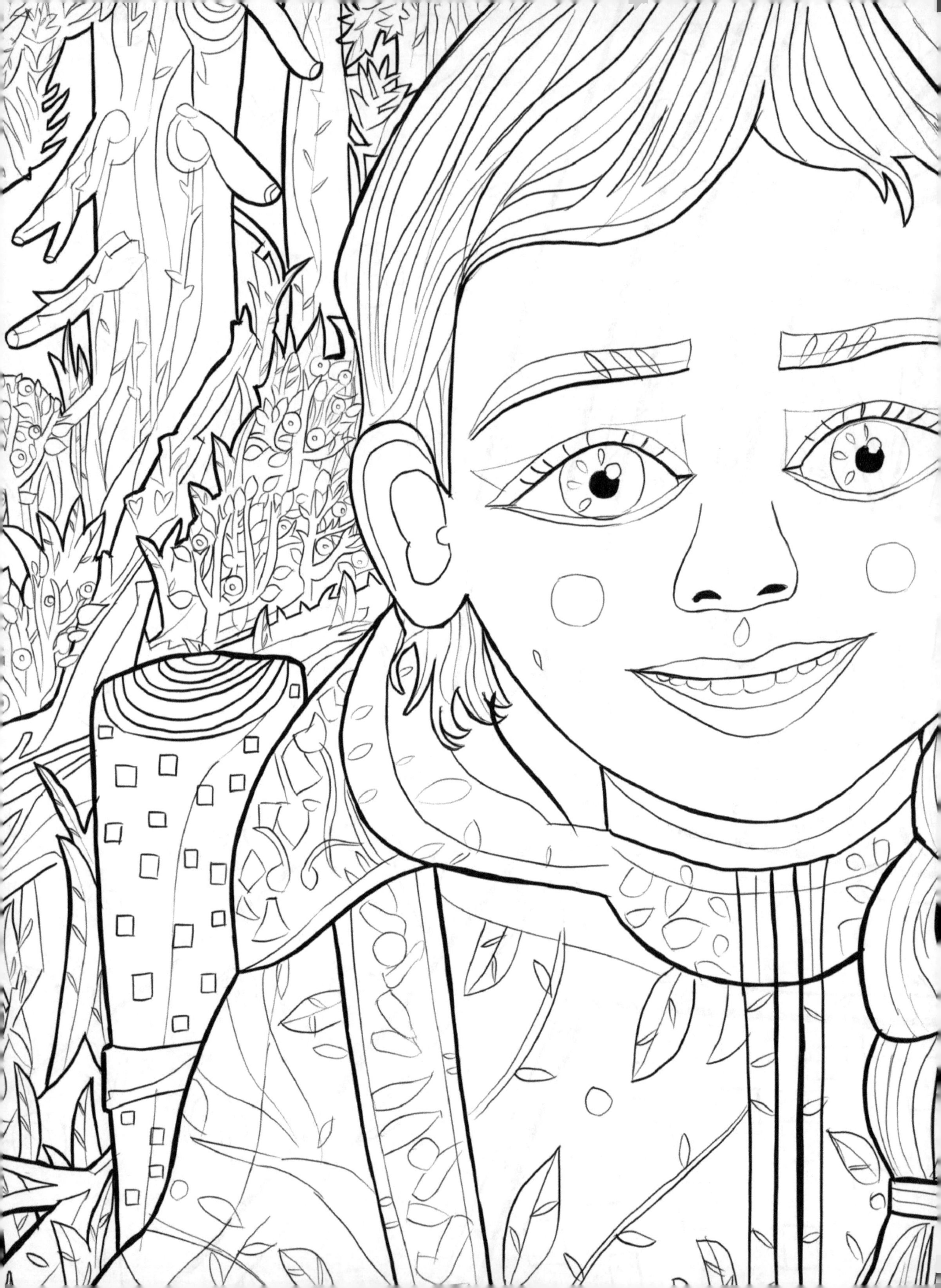

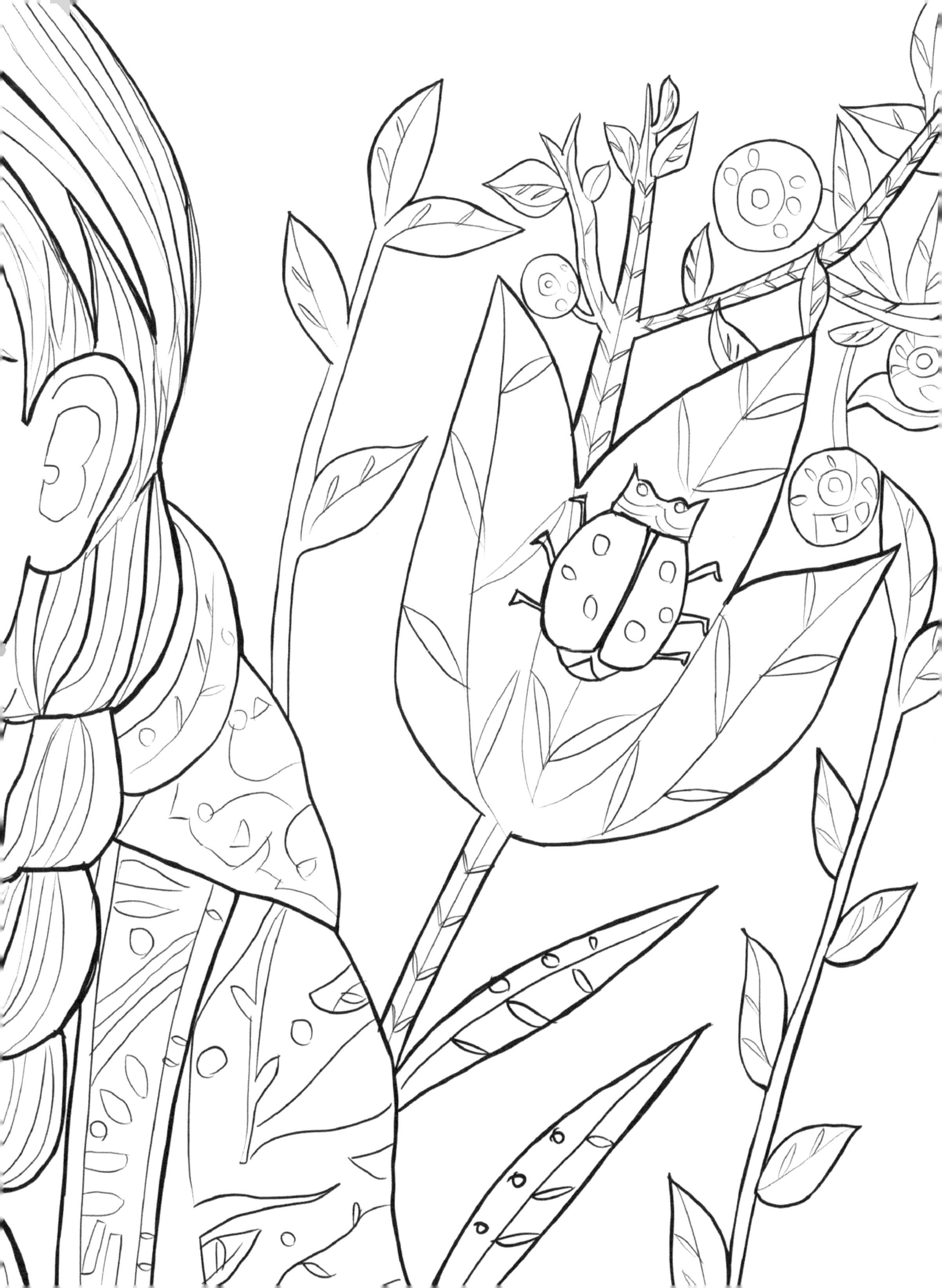

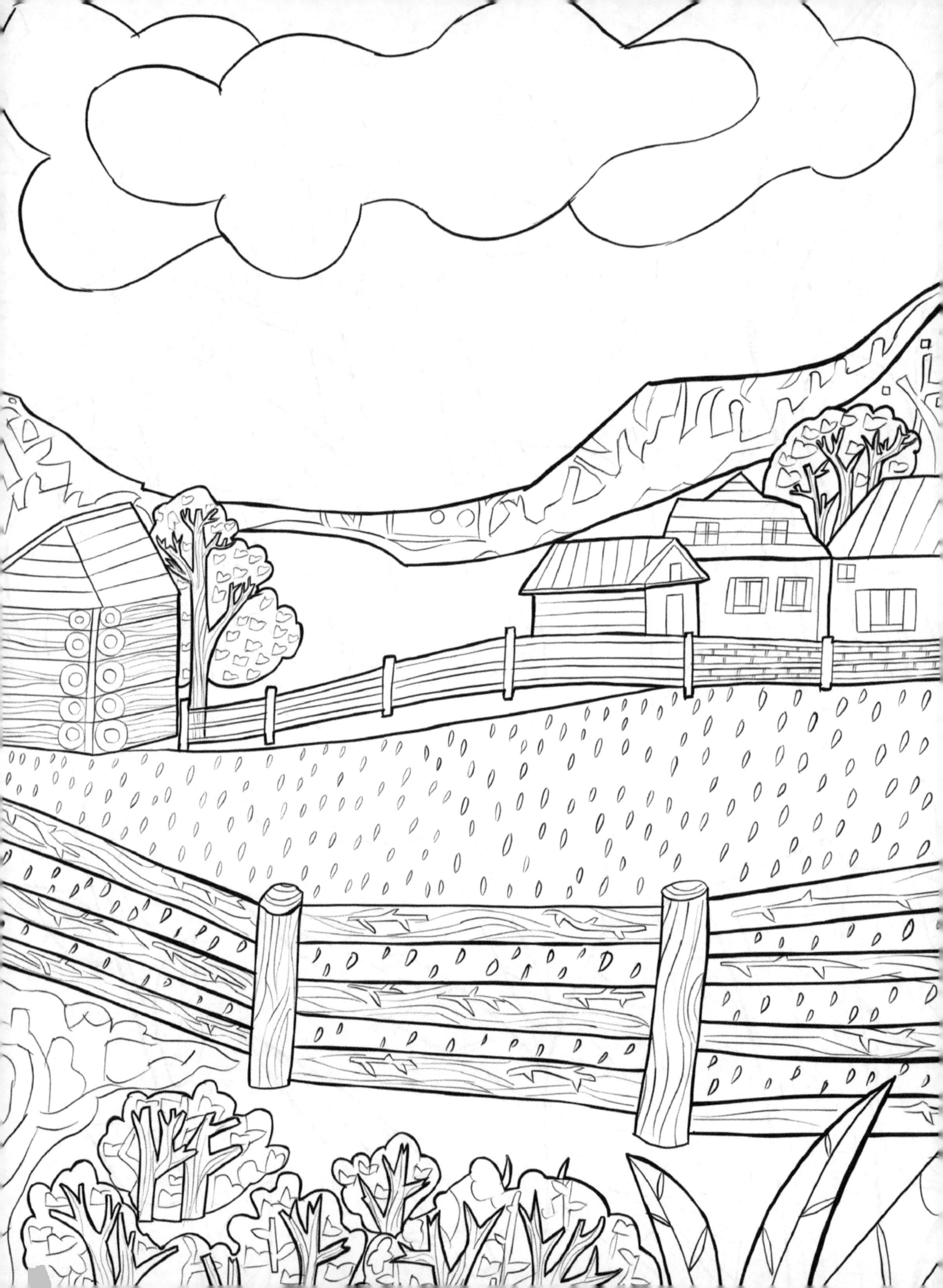

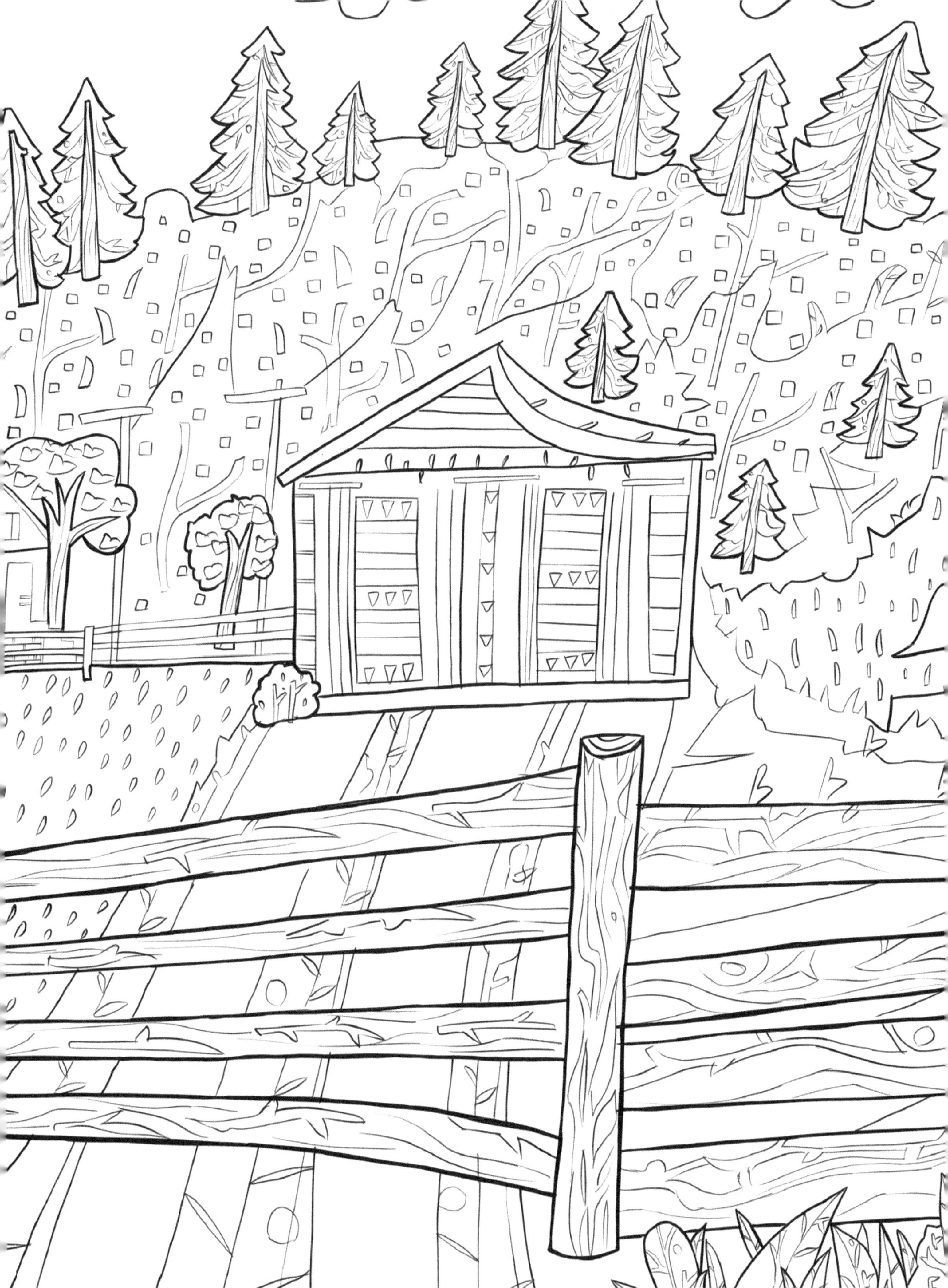

Imprint Wonder River

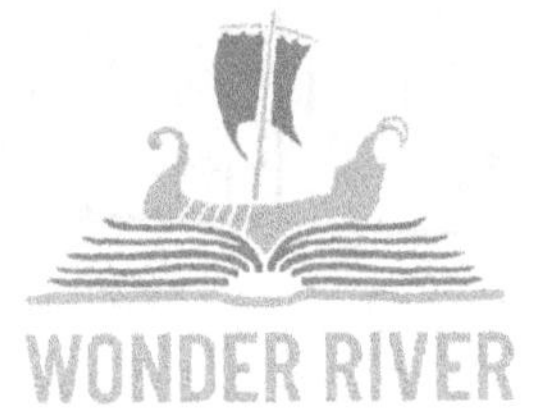

ISBN 979-8-9893510-0-8

Drawings by Tanya Kornienko

Visit the author's website at www.tkart.es

www.ingramcontent.com/pod-product-compliance
Lightning Source LLC
LaVergne TN
LVHW081425110826
845149LV00010B/1868

* 9 7 9 8 9 8 9 3 5 1 0 0 8 *